# Human Capital



Matthew Evanoff

ISBN: 9798482780282

Cover Design by Itzel Flores Sanchez

# Contents

## Can Artificial Intelligence Augment Human Capital?

## What Will the Future of Human Capital Look Like?

# What Is Human Capital?

Human capital is the stock of habits, knowledge and social and personal qualities, including creativity, that incorporate the ability to do work and produce economic value. It consists of knowledge, skills and health that people invest in and accumulate throughout their lives to fulfill their potential as productive members of society. Investments in nutrition, health care, quality education, and professional skills contribute to the development of human capital and that is crucial to ending extreme poverty and forming more inclusive societies.

At the recent Spring Conference of the World Bank Group, finance ministers met to discuss human capital, stressing the importance of human capital and jobs for the economic transformation agenda for countries at all levels of development. History and experience show that economic progress is the key to raise the living standards and dignity of people, especially those in poor or developing countries. There is mounting evidence that most countries will not achieve sustainable inclusive economic growth, will not have a workforce ready for the skilled jobs of the future and will not compete effectively in the global economy. One way out of this is through investment in human capital.

Countries suffering from limited or unequal access to health and education resources suffer from a weak economy. For example, some countries offer free higher education to their citizens, recognizing that a highly educated population tends to earn more and spend more, boosting the economy. The underlying logic is that technological change in the economy drives the demand for highly skilled labor and the overall effect is large on inequality, depending on how resillent the higher education performance is relative to higher demand.

A higher average educational level, ceteris paribus, is intended to reduce the inequality of income by enabling a larger proportion of the population to benefit from higher-skilled activities, according to the results of Sylwester (2003) of OECD countries (an extended sample of countries covering the period 1970-1990 ). But, while there is agreement that there is a positive economic return to education in terms of income levels, theoretical predictions of the inequality effects of changes in enrollment are not straightforward. HDI shows that high levels of human capital education, health and education and per capita income in some countries (e.g. Canada, the U.S.) have linear returns while in others it is less effective.

Human resources are transformed into human capital through the effective use of education, health, and moral values. The transformation of human resources into productive human resources through these effective inputs is the process of human capital formation. Human capital is considered the economic value of thinking, thinking, knowledge, skills, judgment and ability of individual employees [i], and is a key factor in talent management.

Human capital is an intangible asset that is not listed on a company balance sheet but includes things such as employee experience and skills. The economic value of workers' experience and skills include assets such as education, training, intelligence, skills, health and other things that employers value, such as loyalty and punctuality. Employers can improve human capital by investing in education and training that benefits their employees, since not all work is considered equal.

A variety of employee evaluations and human capital management surveys can help to identify gaps in training, resources, job satisfaction and other things that affect workforce effectiveness. An organization's knowledge, skills and capacities are available at all times and are available to achieve positive results, but all management practices must tap into the Human Capital pool in a way that influences the attitudes, behaviors and desired organizational goals of individuals and groups. Calling people "employee capital" may seem like a harsh joke, owing to the similarity of the word capital with cattle, but it can help an organization change its perspective and view employees as assets of increased value.

The concept of human capital originates from an economic model, human capitalism, that emphasizes the relationship between improved productivity and performance and the need for continuous, long-term investment in the development of human resources. In this broad-based model, investment in human capital is seen as impacting national and global economic performance, and investment in people is seen as critical to an organization's performance. Human capital is a hackneyed figure that takes an abstract idea of investing in your employees and transforms it into something that can be expressed in the business success that human capital can drive.

In the 1960 s, the term Human Capital was popularized by two American economists Gary Becker and Jacob Mincer who used it to describe the combination of skills, knowledge, experience, habits, and personalities which each of us uses productively. Human capital is beneficial not only for the person concerned but also for the company they work for and the country that will benefit from it. Back then, people did not know what it was, what capital was, or for whom it was intended.

Economists and businessmen are beginning to consider employees not as interchangeable units that routine tasks do, but as knowledge workers with specific skills and talents that fuel economic growth. In companies, this is called talent management or human resources departments. The Internet has changed the way employers and managers work and work together.

## What Is Human Capital In Economics?

Human capital is critical to understanding macroeconomics. This is because educated people are able to be more productive in the workplace. To do a lot of work and achieve something at the end of the day is rewarding. Workers are trained to be productive for the sake of their moral and spiritual well-being.

The concept of human capital derives from an economic model of human capital that stresses the relationship between improved productivity and performance and the need for continuous, long-term investment in human resource development. Human capitalism recognises that a key factor in performance depends on an adequate supply of high-quality human resources and management strategies that focus on quality, productivity, and working patterns in an organisation to promote these objectives. This model is widely used because investment in human capital is seen as influencing national and global economic performance, and investment in people is seen as critical to an organization's performance.

Human capital consists of knowledge, skills, and health that people invest and accumulate through their lives to fulfill their potential as productive members of society. The model of human capitalism argues that the main source of productive capacity in an economy or organization is a human capacity. Investments in nutrition, health care, quality education, and professional skills contribute to the development of human capital and these investments are key to ending extreme poverty and creating a more inclusive society.

At the recent World Bank Group Spring meeting held in the UK, finance ministers met to discuss human capital, highlighting the importance of human capital for the agenda for jobs and economic change in countries at all stages of development. There is mounting evidence that countries will not achieve sustainable inclusive economic growth without strengthening their human capital, will not have a workforce prepared for the skilled jobs of the future and will not effectively compete in the global economy. For employers, investments in human capital include commitments to training workers, training programs, training bonuses and benefits, family assistance funds, and higher education scholarships.

Economists view spending on education, training, and medical care as investments in human capital. These investments are called Human Capital, because people do not separate their knowledge, skills and health assets in the same way they separate their financial and physical assets. Education and training, along with health, are among the most important investments in the human capital category.

At the same time, a well-educated population is better placed to address other problems that arise in society. The training of workers is seen as very important and many private companies offer training programs. A key advantage of a stable growth environment is that countries can develop high-quality human capital in health, science, management, education and other areas.

At the same time, governments have put more emphasis on education to boost economic growth. For example, some countries have offered free higher education to their citizens, recognizing that a highly educated population tends to earn more and spend more, boosting the economy. A higher average education level, ceteris paribus, should reduce the income inequality by enabling a greater proportion of the population to benefit from highly skilled activities, as shown by Sylwester (2003) in the results of the OECD country sample for the 1970-1990 period.

Although there is agreement that there is a positive economic return to education in terms of income levels, theoretical predictions of inequality effects from changes in enrollment are not straightforward. The underlying logic is that technological changes in the economy drive up demand for highly skilled labor, so the overall effect on inequality is large and depends on how resilient higher education performance is relative to increased demand.

Human capital is a loose term referring to the level of education, knowledge, experience and skills of employees. Human capital theory says that companies have an incentive to seek more productive human capital by adding human capital to their existing employees. Cumulative growth in the formation of human capital generates a high-quality workforce for future generations compared to previous generations.

Human capital is a stockpile of habits, knowledge, and social and personal attributes, including creativity, that embody the ability to do work and produce economic value. Human capital theory is associated with the study of human resources management, but it is also found in the practice of business administration and macroeconomics. In other words, the concept of human capital recognises that labour and capital are not homogeneous.

HR departments can calculate the value and impact of human capital compared to profitable investments based on factors such as the amount of money a company invests in education and training of its employees. Human resources departments that fully understand the importance and value of human capital can produce reports and analyses that promote a deeper understanding of a company's human capital. Human capital research is an evolving process, but a recent study by Matthias Regier and Ethan Rouen examines the importance of understanding the complex relationship matrix between employee spending and corporate performance from the point of view of managers.

In companies, they are called talent management or human resources. In an economy, the term refers to how its population contributes to wealth creation. The production factors are the four inputs required for the production of goods and services.

Capital refers to things that are made by humans, that are made by other things like machines and devices. The term refers to the things that people use to make them productive.

Economic growth depends on the synergy between the new knowledge and human capital: when large increases in education and training are accompanied by great advances in technology knowledge, a country can achieve significant economic growth. But new technological advances are of little value if the country has few skilled workers who know how to use them.

# How Can We Calculate Output Using Human Capital?

The Human Capital Index (HCI) measures the contribution of health, education, and productivity to the next generation of workers. Countries can use the HCI to assess how much income they have missed because of the human-capital gap, and how quickly they can turn it into profits if they act.

The return on human capital is a cost-based measure that reflects the return on investment for people in the form of incremental revenues in which an organization is able to generate an additional dollar per investment per worker. It is one of the three advanced productivity indicators that take into account personnel costs in relation to corporate performance, turnover and profit.

Those indicators can inform the simple formula for investment in human capital. For example, if Company X invests $2 million in its human capital and generates a total return of $1.5 million, managers can compare the return of their human capital year after year to track the return and improve its relationship with human capital investment.

Labour productivity is the value an employee creates per unit of his or her input. If you use input, i.e. How many units of time or how many good books or hours a professor, teacher or lecturer has, then try to measure the market value of that input. One common method of measuring human capital is to try to compare individuals at different skill levels and look at the differences and use these differences as a measure of a worker's human capital relative to others.

The rate of growth of productivity is the primary determinant of an economy's long-term economic growth and higher wages. Productivity is the value an employee produces per hour worked, measured by GDP per hour worked. An economy is at its highest in terms of productivity when the rate of growth of productivity is linked to the rate of growth of its per capita GDP, even though the two are not identical.

Human capital has a perceived relationship to economic growth, productivity, and profitability. Growth accounting tools tell us that changes in an economy's real gross domestic product (real GDP) are due to changes in available capital, labor, human capital, and technology. We can measure output growth, the growth of the capital stock and the growth of working hours.

Because people come from a wide range of skills and knowledge, human capital can help boost an economy. Like other assets, however, it can lose value due to long bouts of unemployment and the inability to keep pace with technology and innovation. Investments in nutrition, health care, quality education and professional skills can contribute to the development of human capital. This is crucial to ending extreme poverty and creating a more inclusive society.

There is mounting evidence that countries will not achieve sustainable and inclusive economic growth without strengthening their human capital, will not have a workforce for the highly skilled jobs of the future and will not effectively compete in the global economy. For these reasons, it is essential to understand and quantify the impact of human capital value and risk on businesses as they attempt to overcome the COVID 19 pandemic.

We have created this guide as a guide to the ROI of human capital, explaining what it is, how it is calculated, and how it can be used to make better decisions in talent management. The ROI of human capital is a leading metric that can change the measurement, control and optimization of labor productivity.

Based on factors such as the amount of money a company invests in education and training its employees, Human Resources departments can calculate the value and impact of human capital by comparing the profit-making investments made. The return on investment (ROI) for human capital can be derived in addition by dividing the total return by the total investment. Human resources departments that fully understand the importance and value of human capital can produce reports and analyses that promote a deeper understanding of human capital business.

Technological change is a combination of inventions, advances in knowledge, and innovations that feed these advances into new products and services. In the 1970 "s for example, half of the US had at least a high school diploma; by the early 20th century more than 80% of adults had completed high school. The Company has increased the level of capital per person as a result of what is known as capital deepening.

Investment in nutrition, health care, quality education and professional skills contributes to human capital development and is key to ending extreme poverty and creating a more inclusive society. At the recent Spring meeting of the World Bank Group, finance ministers met to discuss human capital, stressing the importance of human capital for the agenda for jobs and economic change in countries at all phases of development. There is mounting evidence that they will not achieve sustainable economic growth unless they strengthen their human capital, have a workforce prepared for the skilled jobs of the future and will not be competitive in the global economy.

Despite unprecedented progress in human development over the last 25 years, serious challenges remain for developing countries. In a globalised world economy, human capital is the main factor for intensive development in countries that make forward-looking investments in human capital. Human capital is organised to its advantage in these countries by creating good working and living conditions.

Between 1995 and 2002, Sterlacchini (2008) found that human capital in the form of higher education and the knowledge base had a significant positive impact on economic growth in twelve EU15-partner countries. This paper attempts to assess the impact of human capital on education, health, and economic growth. The analysis of human capital deals with skills acquired through formal and informal education (school and home education), experience and mobility on the labour market.

Cuaresma, Doppelhofer and Feldkircher (2012) used a dataset of 255 EU regions to analyse their 48 potential determinants that explain economic growth between 1995 and 2005. Benhabib and Spiegel use transnational estimates of the physical and human capital stock indicators and perform the balance of growth regressions implied by the Cobb-Douglas production function. To learn how to compare economies with regard to the following steps, follow the work on IT features.

Interest rates and compound interest behave in a similar way to productivity rates. The cumulative growth of human capital formation generates a high-quality workforce for future generations compared to previous generations. Human resources are transformed into human capital through effective inputs such as education, health, and moral values.

The transformation of human resources into productive human resources with effective input (education, health and moral values) is a process of human capital formation. Becker [4] notes that investments in boosting physical and mental health of the workforce are significant investments in human capital and that the root cause of the welfare disparities between nations is the difference between the formation of human capital in countries without physical capital and those with one. The shortage of physical capital in countries with surplus labour can be solved by accelerating the formation of human capital through private and public investment in the education and health sectors of their economies.

Unlike Malthus, economic growth cannot be eliminated by population growth. There are many studies that explain the determinants of human capital and its impact on growth since 1980 [5-10]. Among these studies, other studies mention the importance of human capital for economic growth from the outset and its articulation in growth theory in the mid-1980 "s.

The economic value of an employee's experience and skills includes assets such as education, training, intelligence, skills, health, and other things that employers value, such as loyalty and punctuality. A well-educated workforce is more mobile and adaptable to learn new tasks and skills and to use a wider range of technologies and sophisticated equipment, including those that are creative, forward-looking and improve work management.

In companies, they are called talent management or human resources. Physical capital includes assets and equipment used by businesses and infrastructure like roads and other parts of transport networks that contribute to the economy. In the long run, hourly productivity is an important factor in an economy's average wage level.

Advocates of early childhood education often emphasize the economic benefits of preschool programs, but it can be difficult to win support for these programs because the economic benefits are long-term.

# The Dynamics Of Human Capital Development In Economic Cycles

The Ramsey, Cass and Koopmans model is one of the fundamental models of economic growth theory where representative actors choose a savings rate that maximizes discounted consumption. When considered a closed economy, the RCK standard model has a representative budget that provides labour and capital for the production of one single product and representative enterprise.

In the tradition of the agent-based model [34-40], we introduce a heterogeneous agent model, using agents who follow simple codes of conduct. In the original model, the return on capital on wages corresponds to marginal returns on materials (Methods, Eq.

The partially used index makes it possible to use it as a transitional key to compare the dynamical time series of human capital development in early industrial and postindustrial knowledge and information cycle economic development. The original model is a dynamic system of one-dimensional consumption in which consumption is a deterministic function of the total capital of heterogeneous actors, while the model is two-dimensional in which the total consumption depends on N households called heterogeneous capital k i. The time scale of the model determines the depreciation parameter d, which is the average of its endogenous dynamics, depending on several parameters such as network size and network topology.

In many of the studies examined here, the educational variable (i.e. The proportion of adults in secondary and tertiary education over an average school year) is introduced as a control variable to measure the development of human capital. None of these studies suggests a positive correlation between inequality and the unequal effects of education on income and income inequality, and the studies examined here are largely compensatory. As a result, important policy considerations can be drawn from transnational studies on the multiple causes of inequality.

Access to education and the accumulation of human capital are important factors that are expected to have a negative impact on the income distribution. An above-average education, ceteris paribus, is expected to reduce inequality by enabling a larger share of the population to benefit from highly skilled activities, as demonstrated by the results of Sylwester (2003) for OECD countries, an extended country sample covering the 1970-1990 period. The components of the HDI, namely the life expectancy index, the education index and the income index are linked to the development of human capital in a nation.

HDI is another indicator that correlates positively with the formation of human capital and economic development. HDI shows a higher education of human capital with a good level of health and education, as well as a higher per capita income within a nation. As a result, HDI rates are rising with higher rates of human capital formation in response to higher education and health standards.

Human capital influences economic growth by contributing to the development of the economy by increasing people's knowledge and skills. These skills provide economic value, and a well-educated workforce leads to higher productivity. Consumer spending and business investment not only boosted economic growth but also played a prominent role in determining workers'"levels of education and development".

Recent US research shows that geographical regions that invest in human capital and the economic progress of immigrants living in their countries can help boost their short and long-term economic growth. Human capital is the backbone of human development and economic development in a nation. Human resources can be transformed into human capital through effective inputs such as education, health, and moral values.

The Development of American Economy Program
This program to the development of the American economy examines the causes of long-term growth

and fluctuations in the American economy. Development of economic programs This program examines the forces contributing to economic development in the developed countries. It examines the role of decision making by households, businesses and governments, the impact of development aid policies and the impact of rising incomes in emerging economies.

It also takes into account transport costs, customs duties and other factors influencing geographical specialisation and trade flows. The programme examines aspects related to employment and remuneration including supply and demand for labour and human capital, as well as the factors and consequences of unemployment. It also takes into account the impact of trade unions and policies such as minimum wages and training programs.

In this section of our web you will find a comprehensive analysis of gaps in cognitive and non-cognitive abilities. I am developing a balance model with a smooth occupational reconciliation that includes the accumulation and devaluation of skills, the heterogeneity between workers and companies, and coordinated life-cycle profiles of declining occupational mobility. Each activity is tailored to the individual abilities of the children, whether difficult or light, in order to keep the level of difficulty in which the children learn the most within the zone of proximal development.

These estimates are based on standard ACE models that can be used to estimate inheritance (see Kohler et al. For example, see Krueger and Johnson (2008), which show that parental style influences personality heritability. A caveat should be applied to the indirect impact of economic growth on family instability, which could lead to a deterioration of the human capital sector in society.

# How Countries Invest In Human Capital

Not surprisingly, MENA countries' HCIs vary widely between 0.67 in the United Arab Emirates (UAE) to 0.37 in Yemen. In conflict-affected countries such as Iraq and Yemen, the low indices raise important questions about supporting the protection and improvement of human capital in the midst of conflict.

Although the empirical puzzle has not shown a clear positive correlation between human capital and economic growth, it seems that measurement challenges contribute to the results. This includes taking into account the quality of human capital and the inclusion of other dimensions such as health, social networks and human capital. The components of the HDI, namely the life expectancy index, the education index, and the income index, all relate to the formation of human capital in a nation.

Human capital influences economic growth by helping an emerging economy expand its people's knowledge and skills. These skills provide economic value, and a well-educated workforce leads to higher productivity. The HDI increases with higher education of human capital in response to higher education and health standards.

In the course of training the workforce, another type of investment is capital investment, such as investment in equipment in human capital. Human capital is strongly correlated with economic growth, as investment tends to increase productivity. Consumer spending and business investment not only boost economic growth but also play a prominent role in determining workers' education and development.

Investing in human capital relates to education, and involves, among other things, inculcating values that parents say are healthy, such as nutrition. Just as investing in physical capital, such as building new factories or upgrading computers pays off for businesses, so does investing in people.

The only improvements in the incomes of the top earners point to an increase in income inequality. The incomes of the most educated people are higher than those of the broader population. Improvements in the regions where data by income level is available are due to improvements in health care, reflecting better survival rates for children and adults, lower disabilities and higher school enrolments.

It judges that they have failed to ensure that millions of children in their early years have the nutrition, health care and education to prepare them to take up skilled jobs later in life. The new measure from the World Bank, known as the Human Capital Index, measures youth unemployment, schooling and health in an effort to get countries to step up efforts to ensure that healthy, educated and resilient populations are equipped for the jobs of the future, said the bank. The World Bank said that increased investment in health and education has led to more children being born each year, doubling their lifetime income.

The role of the state is key to raising the skill and education levels of a rural population. Human resources can be transformed into human capital through effective inputs such as education, health, and moral values.

Second, since the outbreak of the pandemic, many MENA countries have shown a keen focus on protecting human capital by increasing cash transfers and strengthening the social security net. Human capital is divided into three types: 1) knowledge capital, 2) social capital and 3) emotional capital. Many theories relating investment in human capital to the development of education are cited and the role of human capital in economic development, productivity growth and innovation is often cited as justification for government subsidies for education and training.

It is of course part of the East Asian region where development success is associated with a focus on human development in the early stages of development. The average among ASEAN countries is undoubtedly fair, but the human capital index, which is expected based on their income levels, suggests that the region still has plenty of room for improvement. We look forward to working together with ASEAN development partners to use the ASEAN community as a test ground to build on our knowledge and improve the human capital level.

Becker's framework is needed to make the importance of education clear and to place people at the centre of the economy. But as a discipline, I object that he overestimates the importance of learning.

Kim Kim described Nigeria which appears on the bottom 10 in the bottom 10 as an example of an oil-rich country that has neglected its education system. According to a new analysis by the World Bank Group, COVID-19 threatens to rebuild some of the gains made in health and education in poor countries over the past decade.

Investing in human capital - the knowledge, skills, and health that people accumulate throughout their lives - is the key to unlocking the potential of children and improving economic growth in every country. The analysis shows that, prior to the pandemic, most countries made steady progress in building human capital, especially for children, with the greatest progress in low-income countries. The Group's 2020 Human Capital Index includes data from 174 countries on health and education - covering 98% of the world's population by March 2020 to provide a baseline for children's health and education before a pandemic.

The UK's actual human capital stock is estimated to have increased by roughly ten times the national GDP from £1.875 trillion in 2004 to £2.14 trillion in 2018. The return on the accumulation of human capital can take various forms, such as increasing labor productivity and economic output, especially in high-income countries.

# The Asymmetric Impact Of Human Capital On Economic Growth

In both cases, human capital rose in response to human capital and total energy consumption in the first half of the period but became more stable in the second half. It remained neutral to changes in renewable energy generation and overall electricity use.

In short, human capital and financial development are the two needs needed to accelerate the growth of emerging economies. Emerging economies should invest in human capital first and focus on financial development second. The results of this research show that both increase economic growth in emerging markets.

The aim of this study is to examine the significant contribution of human capital and openness to trade to economic growth in Asia. In this respect, the literature to date has focused on country and company levels to examine the strong relationship between interest variables. The results of the study show that financial development has a positive and statistically significant effect on economic growth.

In this context, researchers have examined key factors that determine life expectancy and health performance indicators in individual countries. However, the limited literature has shown no relationship between Asian countries and their regions. This study compares economic growth in two different panels of Asian countries based on trade openness and economic growth.

While some empirical studies have identified important factors for health outcomes of the BRICS countries such as health spending, health systems, health care funding and GDP, none of these studies has examined the impact of investment in human capital and technological innovation on the health outcomes of the BRIC countries. One of the main objectives of this study is to examine the dynamic impact of these investments and technologies on health outcomes in the BRICS countries between 1991 and 2019. The study investigates the asymmetric effect of human capital investment and technological innovation on population health over a period from 1991 to 2019 using a panel of BRIC countries.

The aim of this study is to examine the empirical effects of the opening of trade on the growth of gross domestic product (GDP). Essentially, knowledge spill-over effects affect the relationship between trade openness and GDP growth through different measures of the latter. However, the researchers did not give trade openness the externalities that merit scientific attention.

The published literature has examined the positive effects of labour productivity on the opening of trade

[9, 10]. By contrast, trade helps to boost economic growth in countries that have a minimum HCA threshold. As a result, trade effects are complementary, with a higher level of HCA having a greater impact on both trade openness and GDP growth.

Moreover, endogenous growth theory confirms the predominance of knowledge, innovation, and human capital in its contribution to economic growth. Specification 3 shows a significant impact on the long-term economic performance of renewable energy generation by human capital on total energy consumption. ARDL's long-term results show that public-sector education spending tends to influence life expectancy in BRICS economies.

Table 4 reports on the non-symmetric and asymmetric causal relationships between the affected variables in the BRICS economies. Inflation and government spending are negative and have a significant impact on economic growth.

The Lagrange multiplier test and its application to the model specification and econometrics, by Breusch TS, Pagan AR (1980). Hanushek EA, Woessmann L (2008) The role of cognitive skills in economic development. Castello-Climent-Hidalgo-Cabrillana A (2012) The role of quality and quantity of education in the process of economic development.

Check out the updated Human Capital Index 2020 with our video visualizations, frequently asked questions, and more. Nonneman, W., Vanhoudt, P. (1996) Further development of the Solow model for empirical economic growth in OECD countries. M. M., Heston, A. (1988) A new series of international comparisons of real product price levels estimated for 130 countries between 1950 and 1985.

With a focus on human capitalism, an organisation will recruit and compensate the most qualified staff possible, invest in their development, effectively manage them, and, if possible, retain them for the long term. Companies invest in human capital, for example through education and training, which enables improved production quality. Human resources are promoted and achieved through mutual commitment and material investment, and the favor of organizations is reciprocated by their members through higher performance.

The concept of human capital derives from an economic model, human capitalism, which emphasizes the relationship between increased productivity and performance and the need for ongoing, long-term investment in the development of human resources. Human capital theory is associated with the study of human resources management and is found in the practice of business administration and macroeconomics. In this broad-based model, investment in human capital is seen as impacting national and global economic performance, and investment in people is also seen as critical to an organization's performance.

Human capital is an immaterial asset that is not listed on a company's balance sheet but includes things like employee experience and skills. Because work is not considered equivalent, employers can improve human capital by investing in education and training that benefits their employees.

Human capital is divided into three types: 1) knowledge capital, 2) social capital and 3) emotional capital. Human capital is thought to be related to economic growth, productivity, and profitability.

Adam Smith referred to the idea of human capital in his book Inquiry into the Nature and Causes of Wealth of Nations, in which he explored the wealth of knowledge, education, talent, and experience of a nation. He suggested that improving human capital through education and training would lead to profitable businesses that would contribute to a society's collective prosperity. There are many theories linking investment in human capital, the development of education and the role human capital plays in economic development, productivity, growth, and innovation, often mentioned as a justification for state subsidies for education and vocational training.

This course will cover a range of topics related to human capital. The focus is on the development of human capital and the definition of the role of education in economics and politics by historical, comparative, and current perspectives. Human capital throughout history will bring together contributions from leading scholars in economics, history, labor economics, economics, education, and related fields.

In addition, the literature is extensive on the impact of human capital innovation on economic development and growth in the European region (Fagerberg, Verspagen and Caniel 1997; Rodriguez, Pose and Crescenzi 2008; Sterlacchini 2008; Cuaresma, Doppelhofer and Feldkircher 2012). In this report, human capital theory starts in 1776 and ends in the 1960s when theoretical and empirical foundations of the theory are articulated and established.

For example, Badinger and Tondl (2003) examined whether human capital and innovation (measured by patent applications) had a significant impact on the rate of growth of gross value added per capita in 128 regions between 1993 and 2000. Cuaresma, Doppelhofer and Feldkircher (2012) analysed their 48 potential determinants of economic growth between 1995 and 2005 using a data set of 255 EU regions.

The development of endogenous growth models (e.g. Romer and Romer 1986, Romer 1990, Lucas 1988) in the 1980s and 1990s made the integration of various forms of human capital into economic growth models popular (e.g. Recent contributions to human capital theory which combines with growth theory have been contributed by Galor and Galor-Weil (2000), Galor & Moav (2002), Galors (2005a) and Galors (2012).

My findings are consistent with the increasing importance of cognitive skills acquired in early childhood. We apply our findings to the theory of human capital formation, speculating that the greater importance of physical labor in the nineteenth-century economy has increased the opportunity costs of schooling and depressed the relationship between high education and education compared to the twentieth century.

The long-term context of educational variables such as educational attainment, school years, enrollment rates, and spending on education is at least partially unavailable due to a lack of data. However, there is evidence of a resurgence in effort despite this.

The World Bank Group is increasing its human capital investment in sub-Saharan Africa, with a strong focus on empowering women, leveraging technology to accelerate innovation and other priorities. 79 countries at all income levels will work with the strategic approach of the World Bank Groups to transform their human capital results from January 2021. There are many examples of rapid national transformations of human capital, including in Singapore, the Republic of Korea, and Ireland, as well as specific successes in some of the world's poorest countries.

The Internet has changed the way employers and managers work and work together. Economists and businessmen have begun to see employees as not interchangeable units that can do routine tasks, but knowledge workers with specific skills and talents that fuel economic growth.

# How Human Capital Is Changing In The 21st Century

There is no telling what will be required for the steps and challenges of human capital management of the 21st century.

The World Bank Group promotes economic growth as its top priority in its client countries because it knows that income growth is responsible for 70% of its success in lifting people out of extreme poverty in recent decades. Countries like Korea have seen some of those changes at every stage of human capital development.

Today, it is not only about continuing Korea's impressive record of economic growth and the changing landscape of global capitalism but also about how their citizens - young and old, women and men - share in the benefits of that growth. New and fast technologies, newly defined values, and changing customer requirements are changing the way companies operate in the 21st century. For the first time in history, five robust generations form the workforce, with age groups ranging from millennials to baby boomers working together to achieve their business goals.

Companies above all will need to adapt the fastest.

The best way for companies to meet the challenges of human resources management in the 21st century is to adapt an employment-focused approach to strategic management (Goldsmith, 2003). Organizations should rely on human resources experts to be strong leaders who can help employers and workers meet the challenges of the new century in the workplace. Organizations should consider human resources professionals as business partners and strategic thinkers who can take decisions that move the company forward.

Organizations should adopt a more inclusive approach to human resources management that allows employees to contribute to organizational processes. Social media, the need for community managers, and your human resources team require dedicated employees associated with employee leadership. These managers are tasked with relying on frequent surveys to gather feedback and evaluate the health and satisfaction of the workforce.

In addition, the Office of Personnel Management (OPM) will be able to manage the transformation of human capital. As a result of this much needed transformation, the companies will be forced to manage "human resources teams" of new technologies, manage employees' expectations and ensure that the organization has productive and satisfied employees.

HR departments in the 21st century prefer specialization to a generalized, unified approach to workforce management. Instead, the responsibility falls squarely on the plate of the HR manager, who is spread out among a multitude of specialists in his small jack-of-all-trades team.

With the advent of new technologies we could not fathom a year ago, creative forms of work organisation, alternative means of public services, and increasing dependence on agency workers are redefining the nature of public work. These changing trends are occurring as organizations work to stay ahead of their competition and rethink how they move their businesses forward.

Organizational leaders in the 21st century have difficulty managing human resources due to factors such as the high rate of globalization, technological progress, increased competition, and innovation (Goldsmith, 2003). These rapidly changing trends may seem overwhelming, but organizations cannot afford to ignore them. These trends are not going away and how organizations address them could make the difference between an organization's success and its decline in global markets, industries and competitive markets.

Since such factors impact the function of human resources management in the 21st century, organizations have to deal with a dynamic workforce, a working environment, an organizational structure and new strategies of change management. As organizations undergo transition, there is growing pressure on leaders to ensure effective human resources management to meet the demands of change. In such a climate, optimizing human and intellectual capital is the greatest challenge facing organizations.

The agenda includes proposals for reform of human capital management, strategic manpower management, talent recruitment, continuous learning and agile operations. These are sound management practices that are indispensable to the success of any large-scale state transformation. An essential element standing in the way is the human capital infrastructure of the federal governments.

Federal HR offices tend to be transaction-focused and rely largely on the career paths of caseworkers and specialists, and many HR managers are crushed by the workload that many of them experience. Given the requirements that they must understand and apply, it is no wonder that federal personnel offices succeed to the extent that they do.

Changing strategies, design changes and human resources experts need to take account of changes in today's market and improve companies "ability to develop effective human resource management (HRM). HRM is transforming the way companies treat their employees by addressing their needs and increasing their loyalty and productivity in their assigned positions.

The answers are sought through an analysis of relevant literature and current population and labor data from international countries, drawn from a series of elite interviews the authors have conducted with government officials, individuals, and private organizations since 2006.

## The Relationship Between Human Capital And Technology

Human capital influences economic growth by helping an emerging economy expand its people's knowledge and skills. These skills provide economic value, and a well-educated workforce leads to higher productivity. The quality of health and education, both proxies of human capital, has also had a positive impact on economic growth, particularly in higher education (Arabi and Abdalla 2013).

Accordingly, a country's economic growth is determined by the quality of its human capital: higher productivity is achieved through innovation and rapid technological diffusion in a country. High investment in equipment facilitates technology transfer and industrialisation, which can be achieved in countries with different human capital. The relationship between human capital and technology and economic growth may be simple, but empirical studies have produced mixed results, with different studies using different variables and proxies for human capital to determine growth.

There is literature on how human capital influences economic development and the growth of certain technology generations. Human capital refers to explicit or implicit knowledge of individuals and social persons or groups possessing the capacity to create knowledge, and it is useful for organizational missions. Intellectual capital, human capital (understood as individual and group knowledge), and employees of companies are important for companies "ability to innovate.

Opportunity is the second pillar that helps define the relationship between innovation and human capital. Research has shown that opportunity is one of the most important aspects of investing in human capital, and it shows that the problem does not lie in the number of opportunities available, but in the number of people willing to take them for the following reasons. Innovation generates technological capital because, among other things, it acts as a link between the internal values derived from HC (organisational capital) and the external values associated with enterprises (social capital).

In addition, the literature is extensive on the impact of human capital innovation on economic development and growth in European regions (Fagerberg, Verspagen and Caniel 1997; Rodriguez, Pose and Crescenzi 2008; Sterlacchini 2008; Cuaresma,

Doppelhofer and Feldkircher 2012). For example, Badinger and Tondl (2003) looked to examine whether human capital innovations measured by patent applications had a significant effect on the growth rate of gross value added per capita in 128 regions between 1993 and 2000.

The role of the state is key to raising the skill and education levels of a rural population. For example, universities and industry in Jordan have a reciprocal give and take, with universities providing human capital to industry and opportunities for university students to industry.

As a result of business investment, companies are more productive and GDP growth is rising, because business investment is a key component of growth. On the other hand, industry ensures the economic development of the country and government, but the government does not offer the alleged opportunities offered by universities to industry. Consumer spending and business investments not only boost economic growth, but also play a prominent role in determining workers' levels of education and development.

Throughout history, most technological progress has come from large population centers, where more people can discover things and exchange ideas. Most of the rise in living standards that countries around the world are experiencing is due to increased technological knowledge stemming from research and development.

Technological knowledge differs from human capital in that technological knowledge is a social understanding of the best production methods while human capital is the level of understanding of good production methods which is passed on to the workforce. Examples of technological advances include the discovery and use of herbicides and pesticides in agriculture and assembly line production. Note that the tools and machines themselves are the result of earlier human production.

If we understand that health and education are more important than economic growth, we will appreciate that. Promoting resilience to climate change, pandemic and migration resilience, as well as individual resilience, includes social protection.

## How Businesses Calculate Human Capital

Indeed, human capital encompasses the knowledge, training, professional qualifications, professional qualifications, work experience, and skills of your workforce. The development of your human capital ensures that your workforce is effective and efficient and improves the overall performance of your company. Understanding your ROI will help, but no matter what you invest in, there will probably be something, if not human capital, in your investment number one.

Human Capital ROI (HROI) is an HR metric that measures the financial added value for your workforce through the money spent on it in the form of salaries and other benefits. To laypeople, HR ROI is the amount of profit the company makes for every dollar invested in its human capital compensation. The remuneration includes salary, remuneration, and additional cash benefits issued by FTEs (conditional, fixed-term, and part-time) within the organisation.

You can calculate return on investment (ROI) by dividing net income (gross income) by operating expenses (salaries and benefits) minus the cost of salaries and benefits. This metric can be used to demonstrate the actual dollar return for each dollar spent on employees. When your company makes a profit, it covers all its expenditures and investments in human capital, which refers to the amount of money that your organization invests in the development of its human capital.

The ROI of human capital is a cost-based measure that reflects the return on investment for people in the form of incremental revenue, where an organization can generate an additional dollar for every investment in the workforce. For example, a 2.5% return on investment means that for every $100,000 an organization invests in its employees, it can expect that investment to generate additional $250,000 in revenue.

HR uses the ROI of human capital to measure the ROI of recruitment, training, talent development, and other forms of investment. In general, determining the increased profitability that an investment in human capital brings to a company is a way of determining its intangible value. If a company invests USD 10 million in training human capital and makes a profit of USD 20 million a year, all being equal, the company has succeeded in allocating to certain employees, both intellectual and intangible, an exceptional human capital value that will extend over several years.

At the board level, companies attach great importance to analytics to make decisions about how to nurture talent, find ways to retain talent, and use talent recruitment methods. Board bylaws are growing, many companies focus on human capital and an increasing number of organizations use quantitative analysis to measure their efforts, including strategic risks and rewards. For these reasons, it is essential to understand and quantify the impact of human capital value and risk on a company as it attempts to overcome the COVID 19 pandemic.

The human resources department should fully understand the importance and value of human capital by conducting reports and analyses that promote a deeper understanding of human capital of companies. Based on factors such as the amount invested by a company in education and training of its employees, the human resources department can calculate the value of the impact on human capital compared to the return on investment. If your organization understands the impact it has on improving its employees and the value of each contribution, you can create a competitive differentiator for your business.

In addition, the return on investment for human capital is calculated by dividing the total return by the total investment. Return on Investment (ROI) is a measure of how much money you gain or lose from an investment compared to what you have invested. VOI includes financial returns and takes into account the abstract value of a given financial investment.

For example, in the case of a general increase in productivity, the share of the increase in personnel would have to be isolated in order to measure and calculate the ROI.

In 2018, more and more companies continue to invest in areas such as employee morale, engagement and employee satisfaction, and disruptive new technologies such as teamwork make it easier than ever to measure and monitor human capital performance and culture. For example, a training program that speeds up production in the factory leads to an increase in product volume. So calculate the value of the product by dividing the value in an additional product by the cost of providing training materials.

This includes organisational factors on both a systematic and procedural level, as well as personal factors. There are a multitude of variables that influence how individuals acquire and use the knowledge, skills, and experience they gain. Like all reasonable measures, they focus on narrowing and assessing people's impact on corporate performance.

Employees with professional licences are considered a kind of human capital because they enable professional service companies and others in the industry to do business and create added value. Professional licenses cannot be transferred to third parties and are the property of the individual physician, not the company.

The cost approach is the most common method of assessing and compiling the workforce, but income market approaches can also be used to assess whether the resulting cost approach makes sense. For example, an appraiser could divide the value of a professional practitioner by the cost approach and the number of employees in order to calculate an average value per employee. Many organizations collect KPIs for revenue per employee and profits per employee, which they offset.

Due to different economic situations, etc., different distortions of a company's market value are possible, so it is better to measure it over time with a good linkage basis.

The value that employees create for a company can take the form of intangible assets such as intellectual property, brands, and the like, but most corporate employees create short-term value for their customers (month by month, year by year, etc.). Without any intermediary steps to create intangible assets. The level and nature of traditional capital investment is determined by the work of employees, but there are huge differences in the performance of employees in companies (investment banks, hotels, advertising agencies, etc. ), regardless of whether the assets are material or intangible. Focusing on intangible assets is more difficult for companies than vice versa.

## How Businesses Manage Human Capital

Human Capital Management, also known as HCM, is a collection of processes around recruitment, management, development and improvement to create added value for a company. It is a set of practices and processes that a company uses to find, develop and maximize its workforce. HCM provides HR managers with a framework that helps managers and managers to adapt business requirements to work realities and focus on adding value to employees.

According to Gartner, HCM is a set of human resources and resource management practices in the acquisition, management and optimization categories. While HR systems provide the core HR functions for small and medium-sized enterprises, HCS provides comprehensive applications throughout the employee lifecycle to accommodate organizations at the enterprise level. HCS is applicable to any organization, but it is particularly important for companies with knowledge of employees, because the company is the most important asset to its employees.

To answer these questions, you need to understand the importance of your company's employees. An HCM mindset regards employees as corporate assets in which to invest and maximize their organizational value. The main responsibilities of

HCM fall to the HR department of the company, as it plays a crucial role in recruiting talent, managing employee development and acquisition.

In any industry, it pays to keep track of human capital, especially when it comes to employee satisfaction. It is an important process to ensure that companies deploy the right people at the right time to achieve their business objectives now and in the future. Companies that want to reduce turnover need to understand the root of the problem.

At the organizational level, we found that HR departments that focus on workforce analytics to inform their employees about their decisions are the most effective and generate an average of $775,364 in revenue per employee. Companies that use these practices go beyond human resources management to center employees, attract top candidates, and develop employees to make the organization succeed.

In short, the goal of human resources management is to create and manage the systems, processes and policies needed to recruit, train, retain and empower employees to do their jobs. Human resources managers contribute to the entire business process in some ways - by disseminating policies, such as monitoring employee behavior and ensuring that the organization adheres to employee-related regulatory policies.

A key difference between human resources management and human capital management is that human capital goes beyond HR function and encompasses the entire organizational human resources strategy. Effective human capital management requires that it practices talent management, manpower management, proper performance management, and succession planning. Human capital management can be so comprehensive that it not only comprises HR practices (human resources) but also other work practices and strategies to improve organizational performance.

In the past, HR departments lacked respect and investment, but as companies become more aware of the power of their employees, human capital management has become a crucial component of any business. Human capital management gives workers more control over their careers and encourages them to devote their skills and talents to the employer over the long term.

To be competitive you need to invest and make sure you have the tools, processes, data and skills to make success possible. HRM technology offers the opportunity to deliver strategic workforce optimization for your business. With a view to developing superior human resources, a key competitive requirement is the need for long-term functional and strategic plans for top managers to attract many of the best managers to the HRM function of the company.

Simply put, human capital management is about optimizing and investing in your people to reach their full potential. The aim is to develop and manage the systems, processes and policies needed to recruit, train, retain and empower employees to do their jobs. Human capital management's goal is to achieve the highest return on investment (ROI) for Human Capital Employees in an organization.

Remember that if you differentiate between the two, human resources management does not include the various human resources management tasks, work practices and human resources management skills that improve the performance of the organization.

Human Resources Management (HR) is a strategic approach to managing people effectively within a company or organization so they can help their company to gain a competitive advantage. HR is the product of the human relations movement of the early twentieth century, when researchers began documenting ways in which strategic management of the workforce could create entrepreneurial value.

In the current global work environment, most companies are focused on reducing employee turnover and maintaining the talent and knowledge that holds their workforce together. Human resources departments should strive to provide services that are pleasing to workers and reduce the risk of losing the commitment and psychological responsibility of employees. Initiatives and programs should be evaluated to achieve personalised and effective results for workers.

The same is true of the massive effort to improve the management of people in US industry. Since the Second World War, known as "human management", "human relations", "human resources management," "industrial relations management" or "human resources," companies have spent millions to make their employees more productive, loyal and motivated.

The bookshelves swell with people managing books, and hundreds of new ones appear every year. When it comes to talent management, however, companies are so focused on hiring new people that they ignore those they already have.

In today's world of changing workforces, global competition, advances in information technology and new knowledge and the 2008 global recession, demand for sustainable performance has forced business leaders to evaluate and reassess how they operate and operate. In response, business leaders are using new technologies to change their organizational structure, redesign work, relocate the workforce, and improve work processes.

Responsibility lies with the company as a whole and not with individual managers within the organisation. Managers can help maintain strategies for managing human capital and help themselves by providing positive, inspiring leadership to their employees.

## What Are The Social Dynamics In Play With Human Capital?

Access to education and the accumulation of human capital are important factors for the expected impact on income distribution. A higher average education, ceteris paribus, should reduce inequality in the income by enabling a larger proportion of the population to benefit from highly skilled activities, as shown by Sylwester (2003) results for the OECD countries in an extended country sample covering the 1970-1990 period. We create a multi-level baseline model to estimate the unconditional model of progress in mathematics, we report on the variation due to local positions as opposed to schools, and we estimate the impact of the value of human capital on college ambitions and parents decision with mathematics at the college level in 1994-95, as well as the impact of peers on the intermediate mathematical level and social context.

Although there is agreement that there is a positive economic return to education in terms of income levels, theoretical predictions of the inequality effects of changes in enrollment are not straightforward. The underlying logic is that technological changes in the economy drive up demand for highly skilled labor, so the overall effect on inequality is large and depends on how resilient higher education performance is relative to increased demand.

I would not invalidate the theory of human capital but I remain sceptical about its narrow social significance: it has become the property of the ruling class and is used as a mechanism for maintaining its power and reproducing social inequality. Education, in particular higher education, should be considered as a public and social right, and access to human capital should be determined by an investment approach, but should not be considered as an appropriate tool for explaining the benefits of education to individuals and society. Citizenship is seen as a tool, but concepts like social and cultural capital and habitus are the opposite: if human capital recognises that students who do not complete an education have higher returns on the labour market and that economic capital is equally important, then we should try to give a better explanation of the individual drivers behind higher education.

While the concept of human capital is a neoliberal articulation of labor power, this article seeks to show that the socialization of children in human capital must be criticized as a concrete conceptual and social construction of childhood. We argue that questioning how objectification determines forms of childhood isolates and underpins social relationships, does not eliminate objectified forms of identity, and leaves the mechanisms of objectification untested (Bonefeld, 2014).

Two alternative pedagogical practices are used to provide examples of concrete criticism. A peculiar mixture of poststructuralism and positivism is evident in the main equation that Wyness (2012) postulates at the beginning of his analysis of contemporary culture and childhood. His abstract and relativistic attitude frames the social construction of childhood and enables recurring values of voluntary external action by researchers.

## How Human Capital Is Different Around The World

Based on panel data from 100 countries from 1960 to 1995 Barro (1999), Human Capital Formation was a determinant of economic growth, with the condition that empirical estimates are to some extent sensitive to the extent of international openness, the regulatory environment and the level of public funding allocated to schools, health and other important economic sectors. Dessus (2001) overcame this by setting a growth model that includes variables related to school quality, such as the ratio of pupils to teachers in primary education, estimated from panel data from 83 countries over the period 1960-1990.

A recent OECD study on all OECD countries confirms the difficulty of determining a robust positive effect of human capital on per capita income and productivity levels. In fact, a large part of the difference in the income of workers between nations cannot be explained by the accumulation of any kind of capital. There is a strong relationship between productivity and human and physical capital.

On the other hand, the role of human capital in the income disparities between countries is reduced to the extent that qualified efficiency is reflected in technology, institutions and other aspects of the economic environment. Caselli and Ciccone (2018) point out that there is a limit to how far human capital can go to explain transnational income disparities because the quality of different types of human capital is an imperfect substitute. Limiting cross-border differences in efficiency due to economic conditions that permit imperfect substitution implies that human capital may explain lower income fluctuations than previously assumed in the DA literature.

Macroeconomic measurements of human capital show positive and statistically significant correlations between multifactor productivity time series, cross-country panel data and cross-country regressions when timing effects are included resulting in robust methods for estimating the time when a set of controls are included. These findings are consistent with the literature that shows that the role of human capital in explaining transnational output differences per worker doubles if quantity is excluded. They also suggest that measuring human capital, including quality, increases the role that human capital plays in explaining the transnational differences in output per worker.

This paper estimates 12 dynamic panel data models to assess the impact of human capital formation and other key variables on economic growth in 52 countries over a period of 13 years. Several methodological and empirical contributions are made to bring together groups of countries, reduce measurement errors, reduce omitted variables and distortions, and keep the models economical.

Building on earlier efforts, the World Bank created an indicator of human capital for 195 countries by age and gender, measuring educational attainment, quality of education, learning, functional health, and survival over 1990 and 2016 for 195 countries. Evidence suggests that the response of economic growth to physical capital accumulation, institutional development, human capital formation, and aggregate factor productivity varies to some extent across country groups among other things. There are no comparable, uniform measures for each country that reflect all available elements.

Human capital is acknowledged as the level of education and health of a population and is considered an important factor for economic growth. The World Bank calls for measuring human capital and annual reporting to monitor and motivate investment in health and education to increase productivity. The World Bank estimates the expected years of the "human capital" for each country (defined as the birth cohort whose expected life expectancy is between 20 and 64 years ), adjusted for educational attainment, learning, functional health, exposure period, specific age, a specific gender, specific mortality rate, educational attainment, and functional health.

The United States has natural and physical capital - its forests, factories, farms, and chip factories - which is critical to our success, but securing a large stock of human capital separates us from our rivals. To maximize this advantage and ensure that we do not lose a step, it would be wise for politics and business to focus on America's human capital.

After the work of Lucas (1988 ) was given a central role in the analysis of growth and development for disparities in human capital. Consumer spending and business investment not only boost economic growth, but also play a prominent role in the creation of workers' " education and development levels". The role of the state is also crucial in raising the skill and education levels of a rural population.

Klenow (2000), Rodriguez and Clare (1997), Hall and Jones (1999), Parente and Prescott (2000), and Bil and Klenow (2000) argue that the most transnational output differences per worker are not due to differences in human capital or physical capital but rather to differences in the remaining total factor productivity (TFP ). This evidence does not contradict Rossi's evidence and our general discussion. Previous studies have used the same rate of return for each country, and this rate has not changed over time.

In particular, we are examining the impact of the assumption that all children, regardless of their country of origin, go to school with the same human capital, which is what we have set out to do. We convert regional test results into international test results according to subjects and school levels (primary, secondary and adjacent years). By including all tests in the same test round and breaking down education by subject, this method minimizes the likelihood of test differences depending on time, competence, and data availability at school level, while maximizing the likelihood that test differences reflect the difficulty of the tests.

# Which Investments In Human Capital Boost Productivity Growth?

Governments should be involved in improving human capital, regardless of cost, by offering people higher education. Governments recognize that the knowledge that people gain through education helps developing countries and boosts economic growth.

Workers with higher education and skills tend to have higher incomes, which in turn boosts economic growth through more consumer spending. The underlying logic is that technological changes in the economy drive up demand for highly skilled labor, and the overall effect on inequality is large, depending on how resilient higher education performance is relative to increased demand.

A higher average level of education, ceteris paribus, is intended to reduce inequality in income by enabling a larger proportion of the population to benefit from activities with higher qualifications as shown in Sylwester (2003) results for the OECD countries and the extended country sample for the 1970-1990 period. There is consensus on the existence of a positive economic return to education in terms of income levels, but theoretical predictions of the inequality effects of changes in enrollment are not easy. The results suggest that the correlation between average education attainment and multifactor productivity (the overall efficiency of labor and capital inputs used in production processes) is negative and statistically significant in OECD countries.

Economists believe that investment in education and human capital are important sources of economic growth. The contribution of education to the growth of labor productivity is estimated in various studies at 1.3 to 3.0 percent of the total increase. But despite the growth contributions of education in the past, if we move towards a post-industrial, knowledge-based economy, investment in human capital has become more important than investment in other forms of capital.

Investments in human capital - including expenditures on higher education, staff training, leadership development, performance management systems, employee morale and retention programs, and other organizational development measures - help create and nurture a skilled, skilled, motivated, and productive workforce. There are several compelling economic and entrepreneurial reasons to invest in human capital. People invest in human capital for reasons similar to those of corporations in physical capital and individuals in financial assets when they hope to generate income.

Although the empirical puzzle has not shown a clear positive correlation between human capital and economic growth, it seems that measurement challenges contribute to these results. This includes taking into account the quality of human capital and integrating other dimensions such as health and social networks into the human capital stock. Productivity growth slowed from 2.5% per year between 1995 and 2010 to 0.4% between 2011 and 2015, which worries economists, because productivity is a key factor in economic growth, real wages, and living standards.

Human capital is defined as the amount of knowledge, skills, and other personal characteristics that people have that help them be more productive. Human capital development is therefore not only about individual income and prosperity, but also about behaviour of citizens, and affects the future development of the economy and the standard of living of its citizens.

The role of the state is crucial in raising the skill and education levels of a rural population. The continuation of formal education from early childhood through the formal school system to adult education programs and informal learning and work experience represents an investment in human capital.

The World Bank Group has created the country network Human Capital Project to connect governments that prioritize human capital and channel expertise where it is needed. Our work with countries emphasises the efficiency and quality of policy reforms and the mobilisation of national resources so that countries do not spend more than they spend. Protecting people and investing in them is one of the three most important ways to achieve our goal of ending extreme poverty by 2030 and sharing prosperity in all countries.

Human capital consists of knowledge, skills, and health in which people invest their entire lives in order to fulfill their potential as productive members of society. Individuals, businesses and organisations do better when they contribute to the success of the economy as a whole. Investment in nutrition, health care, education and professional skills contributes to human capital development and is key to ending extreme poverty and creating a more inclusive society.

The Nobel prize winner economist Gary Becker explained the relationship between human capital and economic growth when he wrote: "Economic growth depends on the synergy between new knowledge and human capital and when great gains in education and training are accompanied by great advances in technological knowledge a country can achieve considerable economic growth". Earlier this year, Gallup found that the most important factor for millennials applying for jobs is learning and growth.

These estimates are based on a detailed analysis of data on investment in research and development by individual companies. It should not be forgotten that the contribution of investments in software to productivity growth (12%) should be considered a ceiling on the contribution of research and development expenditure. This is significantly less than the investment in people (19 percent).

Recent research, using models in which growth is endogenous, suggests that the direct and indirect effects of education on growth are large. This type of model uses neoclassical and exogenous growth studies to describe how an increase in investment rates leads to higher GDP level long-term and what impact this growth rate has on GDP.

The backlogs represent other factors that contribute more to per capita growth than an increase in physical capital (the machinery and buildings used to produce the goods it contains). Physical capital includes assets and equipment used by businesses as well as infrastructure (things like roads and other components of the transport networks that contribute to the economy).

Based on the results of previous research, we recommend that the analyses focus on the relationship between labor productivity and reward systems and pay particular attention to the needs of the specific human capital, as it is through human capital that they can create value. HCROI enables a company to improve performance when it expects investment in its employees to yield a specific return in the form of a return and the long-term nature of return on investment in human capital should be taken into account.

## The Effects Of Increasing Human Capital Investment On Poverty

Human capital is important because it increases productivity and profitability. Because work is not considered equivalent, employers can improve human capital by investing in education and training that benefits their employees. Human capital has a perceived relationship to economic growth, productivity, and profitability.

The return on investments (ROI) of human capital is calculated by dividing the total profit of a company by its total investment in human capital. Personnel managers calculate the total profit from each investment made. Human capital is based on an employee's investment in skills, knowledge and education, and investment in this area is calculated.

Human capital is a quality of intangible assets that is not listed on a company balance sheet. The initial human capital (H) level in an HM economy converges with the development of a HL-led economy to a lower level in a stable state. There may be an influx of foreign capital, but that is not enough to break up the critical value of HM and it is not enough to return in the long term to a poverty trap.

In the short term, the health of human capital is helping sub-Saharan Africa to escape poverty. The threshold effect of poverty reduction in the model is the elasticity coefficient of human capital health, which differs from the threshold value. In the growth model, poverty traps are aligned with reality, and developing countries can raise the level of human capital above the critical value of HM to get rid of poverty traps.

The term refers to a general change in the overall distribution of income and refers to the premium that graduates receive compared to those without a university degree. Moreover, increasing competition for skills ultimately rewards the highly skilled, and the natural explanation for rising income inequality is that skills are distorted by technological change (Katz and Murphy 1992). If the level of economic development exceeds the threshold level, the impact of health and human capital on poverty reduction will be deeper and better.

This is motivated by the fact that the college wage premium has increased from 0.3% to 0.6% (see Goldin and Katz 2009) as defined as the median wage log of graduates relative to graduates. Technological innovation, introduced in the 1970 "s, seems to have influenced the economy in other ways as well. Firstly, forms of biased technical change and increased competition for qualifications in the previous section have led to technical changes.

## How Investing In Human Capital Affects Quality Of Life

Another advantage of investing in human capital is the improvement of the corporate culture. Improved employee satisfaction, commitment and communication lead to an improved overall culture.

On average, total human capital costs 70 percent of a company's operating costs. Because of the cost of an employee, many companies do not invest in employee development or plan for their human capital. According to a 2015 report by Talent Mobility Research, more than 40 percent of companies say they do not offer career planning and development.

In order to evaluate investments in human resources, it is necessary to plan the educational and development activities of companies. Investment in education and human resources of enterprises In economic theory, investment in training of workers is the most common evaluation of investment in connection with the analysis of investment in human capital.

A problem occurs when the supply of institutions misunderstands the requirements reflected in the amount, structure and expected total return on investment in human capital of companies.

Human Capital Value Added (HCVA) is one of the indicators of overall efficiency and use of human resources. HCVA has an upward tendency, which means that human resources create added value and value. The basic objective measure of the value of the human capital is the quantification of human capital, which is important for the decisions of financial management of the company.

Human capital is the economic value of the ability and quality of work that affects productivity, such as education. Human Capitalism The concept of human capital derives from the economic model of human capital, which stresses the relationship between improved productivity and performance and the need for continuous long-term investment in human capital development. This model can be applied broadly, as investment in human capital is seen as influencing national and global economic performance, and investment in people is also seen as critical to an organization's performance.

Investment in so-called human capital workers is not separate from the skills and qualities of labor that affect productivity, such as education. In companies, they are called talent management or human resources.

The promotion of human capital is an essential and fundamental component of economic growth and prosperity and is vital to fostering a well-educated population ready, willing and able to meet the challenges of the 21st century. Human capital is recognised as an intangible asset whose quality improves workers performance and benefits the economy.

The United Nations estimates that the proportion of over-65s will double by 2050, while the proportion of children under 14 and those aged 15 to 24 will decrease.

In other words, increased investment in education and health is a global concern that affects every country, even the wealthiest. Finland's decision is not unusual, but it poses a greater challenge for investment in human capital. Investing in human capital is long-term, which means that it may not pay off immediately, but it can be worth the wait.

An example of this approach is our country's engagement in Madagascar under the Operations Series "Investments in Human Capital and Development Policy.". The first operation aimed to support the government of Madagascar by investing in human capital to improve human resources in health and education, the availability and predictability of financial resources in the social sector and the legal protection of women and children.

The World Bank Group has created the country network Human Capital Project to connect governments that prioritize human capital and where expertise is needed. Human capital projects support the expansion of this type of support policy and institutional reforms by working with a range of tools and products to help countries achieve their objectives, for example through human capital, public spending, institutional review and case studies that measure success and innovation at country level.

This is a departure from the idea that human resources are used up by other non-human resources, which the members of an organisation must control in order to ensure compliance with the standards of the organisation. Instead, human resources should be promoted and achieved through mutual commitment and material investment, with the organization favoring and reciprocating its higher-performing members.

According to a new analysis by the World Bank Group, the COVID-19 pandemic threatens to recoup some of the gains in health and education in poor countries over the past decade. But ambitious, evidence-based policies in health, education and social protection can regain lost ground and pave the way for the children of today to surpass the achievements of human capital and the quality of life of the generations before them. Investing in human capital - the knowledge, skills and health that people accumulate during their life - is key to unlocking child potential and improving economic growth in all countries.

## The Effects Of Investing In Early Education On Economic Growth

Although there are significant differences between the categories, long-term research has shown that high-quality licensed care leads to higher education and vocational qualifications for children (Stipek, 2018). Studies have shown, for example, that participation in high-quality early care helps children avoid special school grades, repetition of early parenthood and incarceration outcomes — which entail high costs for governments and society.

Early childhood programs do, of course, cost money, but studies show that the benefits of such programs go far beyond cash gains and savings. Children and long-term parents who participate in such programs are more likely to work, have higher tax revenues and have greater purchasing power that contributes to the economy. The projected benefits far exceed the projected costs, and early childhood programs are considered viable in the long term.

Similar to the findings of the Jamaican study, a number of cost analyses have been conducted suggesting that early childhood programs can have a significant impact on economic growth. This policy briefly analyses the impact of high-quality universal preschool policies on economic growth and concludes that such policies could add up to $2 trillion to the annual US GDP by 2080. Although early childhood education advocates emphasize the economic benefits of preschool programs, it can be difficult to win support for them, given the long-term benefits to the economy.

Economic development begins with early childhood development and the best investment is to ensure that all children have access to a quality early childhood education. Studies show that public expenditure on early childhood education and care (ECE) is the best long-term investment for children. It is clear we should aim for the benefits of investing in high-quality early childhood education for disadvantaged children in order to avoid performance gaps, improve health outcomes, boost incomes and achieve high economic returns.

More ambitious investment in the US's children, for example, would raise average levels of education not only by closing the achievement gap, but also by closing it. There is good reason to believe that universal programs that generate significant benefits will not bring the same benefits to all participants or the same high returns as programs that target disadvantaged children. Instead, most of the benefits go to children most affected by resource scarcity, which improves their economic mobility.

A high-quality universal pre-kindergarten program could cost just $5,800 per participant and is expected to enroll 7 million children by 2017, after which it would expire. In 2017, only 11,800 children would be enrolled in the small state of Vermont and more than

891,000 in a large state, California, after phasing in. Given compensatory spending on Head Start and special education in existing state kindergartens, the universal program would cost just over $6.7 million in Vermont in 2017 and nearly as much (an additional $4.1 billion) in California.

Lynch and Vaghul (2015) estimate over a 34-year period (2016-2050), that the annual benefits of a large investment to provide universal, high-quality preschool education to all American 3 and 4-year-olds would amount to $10 billion. We estimate that from every 100 children, 70 would attend a high-quality, voluntary, universal public preschool program. These children make up half of the children who currently participate in public programmes, half of the children who participate in private programmes and 60% of the children who do not participate in pre-school programmes.

Assuming that children who did not go to preschool in the absence of a universal program would reap 100 percent of Perry's estimated benefits, a full 0.9 years of educational gain. New Jersey's Abbott Preschool program is an important benchmark of high quality and continuous improvement. The program began in 1999-2000 and served children in 31 high-poor towns, of which 19 percent (29 percent in the state) were 3- to 4-year-olds (Barnett et al.)

For example, they found together with the National Forum on Early Childhood Policy and Programs that

High-Quality Early Childhood Programs provide a 4-9% return for every dollar invested. The early years of children are the key to their success and in Arizona, children who are healthy and prepared when entering kindergarten are more likely to graduate and go to college. Educated adults are better prepared for employment opportunities in the global market and contribute to the strength of their communities.

Studies on ECE effectiveness point to quality as a key factor in generating long-term benefits for children. Numerous studies have shown that children who have access to high-quality early childhood education are better suited for kindergarten. Compared to participants in low-quality informal ECE programs, children in high-quality ECE programs experienced higher graduation rates, income and health among male participants as well as additional decreases in interactions with the criminal justice system (McCoy et al.

# How Human Resources Departments Manage Human Capital In Business

Management involves recruiting and hiring people with specific skills to achieve the company's current and future goals, coordinating employee performance and proposing employee training and development strategies. Recruitment is the selection of potential employees through interviews, applications and networking.

The top managers attract many of the best talents in the company with a view to developing superior human resources as a key competitive requirement and the need for long-term functional and strategic plans. Companies shift outstanding managers from HR functions over a period of two to four years to five to seven years, developing top management groups with a high degree of experience in formulating and implementing HR strategies. Talent acquisition, management, recruitment, onboarding and training of top talent are the primary tasks of personnel management.

A group of loyal and productive employees is the organization's most effective competitive weapon. Companies use the practice of getting deep into human resources management to center employees, attract top candidates and develop them so that the organization can succeed.

The main advantage of human capital management is that it provides a process for managing resources of a company. It creates an overall system that the HR department can use to nurture and train the best talent to achieve organizational goals. The biggest advantage of this process is that it enables companies to get the maximum value out of their employees.

The goal of human resources management is to develop and manage the systems, processes and policies needed to recruit, train, retain and empower employees to do their jobs. Remember that if you differentiate between the two, human resources management does not include the various human resources management tasks, work practices and human resources management skills that improve the performance of the organization.

The most important difference between human resources management and human capital management is that human capital goes beyond HR functions and covers the entire Human Resources Strategy of the organization. Human capital management, or comprehensive human capital management, encompasses not only personnel practices, but also other work practices and personnel management strategies to enhance organizational performance.

Effective human capital management requires that it practices talent management, manpower management, proper performance management, and succession planning. To work effectively, HR leaders must rely not only on best practices and management standards and workflows as key factors, but also on the policies that managers set. According to human resources managers, the challenges of human capital management motivate people to do their best which can be challenging and certain areas can be difficult to manage and optimize.

Human Capital Management (HCM) provides HR managers with a framework to help executives and managers adapt business requirements to work realities and focus on adding value to their employees. HCM technology offers the opportunity to deliver strategic workforce optimization for your company. While human resources management systems provide centralized HR functions for small and medium-sized enterprises, HCM provides comprehensive applications throughout the employee lifecycle to accommodate organizations at the enterprise level.

Human Resources Management (HRM) is a term used to describe a formal system designed to manage people in an organization. HRM is designed to maximize the productivity of the organization and to optimize the effectiveness of its employees. HRM focuses on central administrative HR functions such as keeping staff records and managing social benefits.

The second definition refers to the practice of managing people in the workplace, including the general working environment and corporate culture (HRM for short). Learning Objectives Break down Human Resource Management (HRM) Attractiveness Selection, Training, Evaluation and Rewards Key Points Human Resource Management monitors organizational leadership and culture and ensures compliance with labor laws.

When it comes to talent management, some companies are so focused on the hiring of new staff they ignore those that they already have. Recognizing the importance of human resources management for the overall health of an enterprise also applies to small enterprises, although they do not have the same human resources requirements as larger organisations ; nevertheless they face human resources management problems which can have a decisive impact on occupational health. Smaller companies are less able to work with a single HRM specialist than larger companies, which requires a larger HRM team to keep pace with HR management requirements.

The global recession and demand for sustainable performance 2008 forced business leaders to review and re-evaluate their management and operations with a changing workforce, global competition, advances in information technology and new knowledge. Workplaces are less bright, less ventilated and less safe than in the past. In response, business leaders are using new technologies to change their organizational structure, redesign work, relocate workers, and improve work processes.

The term "human capital" dates back to the seventeenth and eighteenth centuries, when economists like Adam Smith sought to quantify the value of labor productivity and income. Over time, human resources research became popular in the academic world, and companies established human resources departments. Economic theory continues to influence human capital management and supports the concept of employee investment and the value of an organization that relies on skilled, productive, and creative people.

# Gary Becker And Theodore Schultz And The Definition Of Human Capital

The Human Capital approach assumes that income is a measure of how much workers have invested in their skills and knowledge, rather than assuming that income differences reflect whether workers have good or bad jobs. According to this approach, revenue increases with the amount invested in education and training. However, it recognises that most of these training-related and general costs are shared between workers and companies depending on each other's attitudes, such as risk, desired liquidity and patterns of labour turnover.

The shortage of physical capital in countries with surplus labour could be solved by accelerating the formation of human capital through private and public investment in the education and health sectors of their economies. Human resources could be transformed into human capital through effective use of education, health, and moral values. Under the human capital approach, the best jobs would be those of workers who have invested a large part of their human capital.

Gary Becker and Theodore Schultz developed the theory of human capital in the 1960s. In the early 1960s, the American economist Theodore W. Schultz coined the term "human capital" to refer to the amount of productive knowledge and skills the workers possess. Human capital is a measure of education, skills and other characteristics of a human resource that affect its productivity potential.

Human Capital Theory developed by the Neoclassical economists Gary Becker and Theodore Schultz is seen as a useful way to explain how employees can increase their value to an organization, leading to improved skills, autonomy and socioeconomic well-being. The theory of human capital was coined by Becker, an American student of Schultz, who treated human capital as a result of the investment process. Because acquiring productive knowledge is costly (students pay direct costs by forgoing the ability to earn a wage), Becker concluded that rational actors make such investments when the expected future income stream exceeds the short-term costs of acquiring skills.

Self-employment, portfolio careers, the gig economy and on demand business models such as Uber and Deliveroo reflect all assumptions of human capital theory. Human capital research is an evolving process, but a recent study by Matthias Regier and Ethan Rouen examines the importance of understanding the complex relationships between employee spending and corporate performance from the perspective of managers. Human capital theory implies that workers bear the costs and benefits of their investments.

This question is at the heart of many contemporary analyses of employment relations. Human Capital Theory (HCT) has long been touted by states and education systems as subservience to the vaunted "knowledge economy" that is crucial to economic growth. But HCT has faced the same problems and limitations as any human capital theory that attempts to explain phenomena: its basic assumptions about human motives, goals and decisions are not well founded, it turns out.

It defines human capital as 'activities that influence future monetary and psychological income by increasing people's resources' (Becker 1994: 11). Its main forms are schools and vocational training, but it also takes into account medical care, migration, the search for information, the prices and the income. Its main purpose in developing this book was to move from an empirical to a theoretical one.

The paper was presented at a conference on human investment organized by T. W. Schultz in Chicago in late 1961 and formed the core of the future theoretical chapter of the books. For economists today, the notion that discrimination is a costly factor of discrimination owes much to Becker. Companies, it said, had talent management and human resources departments.

Why The Human Resources Department Is A Bad Human Capital Management System

Organizational management and occupational psychology contributed to the fact that personnel managers paid more attention to the needs of employees for performance, advancement and recognition, which corresponded to the nature of the work itself and to the abilities and interests of the individuals. As new and emerging technologies moved the focus from human resources management to administrative tasks, today's HR departments - at least the most forward-looking - invested their energy in managing employee engagement and strengthening culture. They were assigned to manage the employees themselves, which increased the likelihood that the employees would be happy at work and stay for the foreseeable future.

Considering that the Human Resources Department is the functional company with the highest authority and responsibility for effective human resources management practices, it has helped several companies attract and retain the best human resources managers. Companies that promote outstanding managers to human resources roles over a period of two to four years (or five to seven years) develop top management groups with a high level of experience in formulating and implementing human resources strategies. The development of superior human resources as an essential competitive requirement and the need for long-term functional and strategic plans attract top managers to the HRM function of companies and many of the best managers.

HR departments today face the biggest challenges in recruitment, retention, motivation, leadership and the development of corporate culture. It has been proven that the management and development of culture through recruitment improves employee retention and performance.

This is changing the role of human resources and shifting more strategic issues to outsourcing functions so that they can manage and grow their business at no cost. HCM (Human Capital Management) refers to cross-functional consulting between human resources departments, marketing, customer service and finance.

Human Resources directs employees to managers to focus on tasks related to improving employee relationships and recruiting new employees. The mission of HR is to ensure managers have the training and resources needed to meet the needs of employees.

Depending on the size of your business, you may face some of these challenges, but don't add a human resources department because you may find that it causes more problems than it fixes. Human resources departments carry out a wide range of tasks, and failure to plan the responsibilities of departments can lead to an unproductive and inefficient workplace. Companies that lack human resources have difficulty building and maintaining solid relationships with their employees.

Employees hate human resources for a variety of reasons, some of which are logical reasons based on poor experiences with a human resources team, but there are other reasons, such as when they show that they lack knowledge of the role of human resources in the workplace.

They are all intertwined, and employees tend to mention at least two or three of them when they complain to their supervisor or department. Despite the complaints and situations of the employees, the staff seems to be on the side of the manager most of the time. For employees, the interests of the company seem to be more important than those of the manager.

If you have multiple witnesses or employees who complain about the same behavior, the HR will side with the company. In its effort to protect the company from lawsuits, the human resources department is covering up legitimate concerns of employees. Illegal questions about potential candidates, managers who do not adapt their management style to the needs of employees, the establishment of salary checks that distort the protected class, and this out of ignorance, endanger staff.

This can lead to blanket liability actions by customers, hacking by third parties, workplace liability claims, repeated injuries to workers and the terrible effects of workers' deaths. In fact, studies have shown that every single lost employee incurs expenses that are multiples of their annual salary. The cost of an unhealthy staff turnover rate can be crippling for an organisation.

Human Resources Management is an area dedicated to training and mentoring employees. While it may seem self-evident that investing in employee training would benefit your employees who work hard and stay in your company, the reality is far from straightforward. Executives in certain departments are tasked with evaluating whether a particular candidate is qualified and suitable, but the HR department is responsible for initial contact and conducting the initial interviews.

Human Capital Management (HCM) in an organization is a comprehensive set of practices for the recruitment, training, and retention of employees and intangible assets through strategic and tactical practices, processes and applications that maximize enterprise value, focus on organizational needs and provide specific skills. There are many similarities between human capital management and personnel management systems. It is important that both deal with the Human Resources Department which is a specialized office within a company or company that deals with the workforce, employees and related issues relating to employment, recruitment, orientation, training, development, payroll, benefits, performance, evaluation, analysis and other work-related services for employees.

In combination with software, Human Capital Management (HCM) helps administrators and business leaders to answer these important questions. HCM defines practices and processes that a company uses to acquire, develop and optimize its workforce. It provides HR managers with a framework that helps managers and managers to reconcile the business needs, the reality of their work and the added value of their employees.

If employees feel appreciated by their employers, they are more likely to recommend them to companies, recruiters and HR managers who do not have to search through stacks of CVs to fill vacancies. The same is true of the massive effort to improve the management of people in US industry. Continuous feedback on the performance of HCM solutions enables managers and employees to work together for better results.

## Is It Possible To Quantify Human Capital?

Many times I have wondered whether it is truly possible to quantify human capital in a productive way. By productive I do not mean the measure of the work product output over time. Sometimes it is a question of measuring objective performance indicators, such as completion of a sale or how much time people spend on various tasks in time tracking apps. Other times it's an assessment of how superior someone is, using a similar score scale or employee satisfaction surveys.

Either way, it is possible to calculate the contribution of employees to the value of the company by comparing their salary and performance. Investing in employees is not the same as buying a device, but you should be able to measure the value they bring to your business. Hiring and training costs can offset the value that an employee brings back to your business.

The ability to quantify how employee performance and hiring costs impact your bottom line is an important part of a robust books management system. Investors are important components of the evaluation and decision-making of human capital value, costs, productivity, demographics, well-being and operational dynamics of human capital, and they need better information.

The company should carry out an independent assessment of the risk of national bonds, bringing into account measures related to human capital such as life markets, and integrate better measures for human capital into credit programmes that recognise the challenges of economic growth in a low human capital environment. This is particularly true for institutional investors, who evaluate investment opportunities that could create long-term value for customers and beneficiaries. For these reasons, it is essential to understand and quantify the impact of human capital risk on companies as they attempt to overcome human capital management and investment challenges.

Decisions are often based on indicators tied to the business's financial drivers such as revenue growth, capital expenditures and excessive capital distribution. In addition, organizations create or reduce value in a number of ways that are not reflected in the consolidated financial statements. This is because they do not take investment decisions into account or promote them.

Indeed, human capital encompasses the knowledge, training, professional qualifications, professional qualifications, work experience and skills of your workforce. Human capital refers to knowledge, skills, experience and other attributes as well as the obligation to invest in an organization, and that is what you should focus on to improve your ROI from human capital. When companies hire employees, they invest in them by recruiting, training, offering attractive compensation packages, raising salaries and much more.

Determining the human capital value of an individual employee can be a challenge. While the economic value of human capital can be measured by individual workers, human capital is also estimated by the economy as a whole.

The ROI of human capital is a cost-based measure that reflects the return on investment of people in the form of incremental revenue, where an organization can generate an additional dollar for every investment in the workforce. For example, a 25% return on capital for human capital means that for every $100,000 of additional investment in its employees, an organization expects the investment to generate about $250,000 in additional revenue.

In general, determining the increased profitability that investments in human capital bring to a company is a way of determining its intangible value. HR leverages the ROI of human capital to measure the ROI of recruitment, training, talent development, and other forms of investment. To quantify intellectual and human capital assets, companies use a modified Return on Investment (ROI) approach.

If a company invests $10 million in training human capital and makes a profit of $20 million a year, when everything is the same, it can assign exceptional human capital value to certain employees, even if the intellectual intangibles are transferred over several years. Measuring human capital represents one of the greatest opportunities for HRs to prove that it is a strategic function. In this first part of a two-part investigation of this research, we present a picture of the current geographic location of human capital in the UK, how it is measured and what companies hope to accomplish by measuring it.

While financial capital is the monetary value of what you own (your net worth), human capital looks like today's assets and liabilities. Personal human capital is more difficult to measure than net wealth or financial capital, because it is based on qualitative rather than quantitative analysis, which requires educated assumptions rather than verifiable measurements. In an article by World Bank President Jim Y. Kim, he notes that, with the right measurement, an index that measures a country's human capital would be hard to ignore, and would help stimulate more effective investment in people.

It allows you to compare your business with your competitors and supports your business planning initiatives. Now that you understand the benefits of using HRCI, you may be curious how to calculate it best for your own business.

They can then compare their ROI results by adding new employees to their payrolls. School leaving certificate is a standard form of meat grinder and a direct measure of school return that summarizes the investment value of a school over time and space. [5] The driving force behind acceptance of school leaving certificates as a measure of human capital is its availability. These findings are consistent with literature that shows that the role of human capital in explaining transnational differences in workers output doubles when quality is taken into account.

## What Is The Difference Between Specific Human Capital And General Human Capital?

It is an intangible asset that is not listed on a company's balance sheet, but includes things like employee experience and skills. Company-specific human capital (FSHC) is an integral part of the vocabulary and strategy of this field.

Human capital is the economic value of the ability and quality of work that is influenced by productivity, such as education. Human capital is thought to be related to economic growth, productivity, and profitability. Because work is not considered equivalent, employers can improve human capital by investing in education and training that benefits their employees.

In companies, this is called talent management or human resources departments. These investments are called human capital, because workers are not disconnected from the skills and qualities of work that affect productivity, such as education.

Human capital theory stipulates that certain skills contribute to the productivity of the current enterprise. It's what makes it special. General human capital consists of education and training valued by various companies, while specific human capital is only valuable for the current employer.

Human capital is a stockpile of habits, knowledge, and social and personal attributes, including creativity, that embody the ability to do work that produces economic value. It is recognised as an intangible asset whose quality improves workers' performance and benefits the economy. Companies invest in human capital, for example through education and training, to enable a higher level of production.

Human capital theory is associated with the study of human resources management and is found in practice of business administration and macroeconomics. The model developed in this paper relies on the theory of Human Capital to explain how start-ups can reach long-term growth and reduce their chances of failure. Based on a sample of 201 business start-ups that were examined for growth and failure over a 12-year period, we find that both specific and general human capital can lead to growth and failure in various ways.

I found that the effect of general human capital on failure is usually mediated by growth. Specific human capital is not linked to growth and has a direct negative impact on business failure.

In his book Inquiry into the Nature and Causes of Wealth of Nations, Adam Smith first referred to the idea of human capital in his book Exploring the Wealth of Knowledge, Education, Talent and Experience of Nations. He suggested that improving human capital through education and training could lead to more profitable enterprises and increase a society's collective prosperity.

Human resources can be transformed into human capital through effective inputs such as education, health, and moral values. The transformation of human resources into productive human resources through these inputs is a process of human capital formation.

Human capital is an intangible asset of a quality that is not listed on a company balance sheet. While investing in physical capital, such as building new factories or upgrading computers, pays off for businesses, investing in human capital pays off for people. These investments relate to education, but include, among other things, the imparting of values by parents, such as healthy eating.

The economic value of the experience and skills of an employee includes assets such as education, training, intelligence, skills, health and other things that employers value, such as loyalty and punctuality.

We should define specificities in terms of the size of the labor market and the skills acquired through training. In view of the fact that self-employed employment decisions can be complex and the fact that the incomes of self-employed workers seem to differ from those of workers, we have decided to exclude this group of workers. Human capital is defined as a specific combination of weighted general skills.

Going back to the origins of human capital, we should review Becker's history once more. With a doctorate in hand, Becker was commissioned by the National Bureau of Economic Research in the mid-20s to work on a project to calculate school yields.

What seemed like a simple question led him to realize that no one had yet concretized the concept of human capital. In the years that followed, Becker developed the concept into a mature theory that could be applied to a number of questions and questions in the fields of economics, marriage and fertility. One of his earliest contributions was to distinguish between specific and general human capital.

As a result of the conceptualization and modelling work of Gary Becker, economist and Nobel laureate at the University of Chicago, human capital was a key factor in awarding the Nobel Prize in Economics to Paul Romer in 2018, who established the modern innovation-driven approach to understanding economic growth. The value of investing in human and social capital in the business development of startups. The dimensionality of organizational performance and its impact on strategic management research.

# How Investment In Human Capital Improves Economic Mobility

The deployment of human capital is essential for the immediate recovery and long-term development of the MENA region, which has the highest youth unemployment rate in the world with over 25%. Strong efforts are needed to preserve the human capital of displaced persons and refugees in order to promote social inclusion and economic mobility. Without human capital investment, economic mobility is severely limited or non-existent.

Human capital refers to the knowledge, skills and experience of workers in an economy. It influences economic growth and contributes to the development of an economy by increasing people's knowledge and skills. Human capital development, education and workforce preparation play a crucial role in increasing the access, opportunities and economic mobility of people on low incomes.

The knowledge and skills of its people provide economic value, and skilled labor leads to higher productivity. The concept of human capital is the recognition that not everyone has the same skills and knowledge. Investment in so-called human capital workers should not be separated from the ability and quality of work that affects productivity, such as education.

In companies, they are called talent management or human resources. Because of the cost of an employee, many companies do not invest in employee development or plan for their human capital. Those who spend money do not pay much more for employee development, just as those who pay a considerable amount for a Super Bowl commercial refuse to spend money to film a high-quality commercial.

Gary Becker realized that investing in workers is nothing more than investing in capital goods or any production factor. According to his research, he has found that people are more likely to pay for a general investment in human capital, but companies are less likely to pay for specific human capital. Businesses are not interested in investing in workers who can be snapped up by their competitors.

Investment in human capital benefits not only individual workers, but also the economy in which they participate. It creates greater earning potential and increases the ability to build wealth, in this case through education. The Beckerss theory explains another way in which investment in education benefits companies, counties, and individuals.

Consumer spending and business investment not only boost economic growth but also play a prominent role in determining workers'"levels of education and development". The process of training the workforce is the kind of investment that is a capital investment, such as an investment in equipment in human capital. Human capital correlates strongly with economic growth, because investment tends to increase productivity.

Education is an important form of investment in human capital and has become a focal point of economic policy. There is evidence that the correlation between average educational attainment, multifactor productivity and the overall efficiency of labor and capital inputs in the production process in OECD countries is negative and significant. This suggests that the better educated and educated a person is, the more productive he or she becomes.

Today's job market requires like-minded people and professional networks to better understand the possibilities of our modern economy. It may not be work for today's children, but they can use their skills and cognitive abilities to get better employment and increase productivity at full UHCI. This lesson applies to all workers, regardless of their level of education, but it is especially acute for low-skilled workers who are more likely to rely on public funds.

Simply put, these challenges underscore how low-income workers are disproportionately disadvantaged in their efforts to attain upward mobility in a knowledge-based economy, such as education, skills, peers and professional networks. The labour force system has not exhausted its potential to help adult workers build up their human capital. It is time for the system to take its place in preschools, kindergartens, elementary schools, secondary schools and traditional four-year colleges to promote education that develops human capital throughout our lives.

The role of the state is key to expanding the skills and education of rural populations. Throughout the twentieth century, America's investment in education has been a major source of its exceptional performance, and a renewed commitment to investment in education is an important and fruitful step that federal, state and local officials can take to sustain American economic growth. There is evidence of positive educational and economic outcomes at public colleges and universities in most states, which receive most of their income from tuition and state funds.

Despite repeated promises by policymakers to spend more on infrastructure and other important investments, US public investment has hit a new low. Chronic disinvestment in Kindergarten and 12th grade has triggered a wave of teacher strikes across America, and the spending levels have not recovered from the deep cuts of the Great Recession.

Although empirical puzzles have failed to show a clear positive correlation between human capital and economic growth, challenges in measuring it appear to have contributed to these findings. This includes taking into account the quality of human capital as well as the integration of other dimensions of health care and social networks into the human capital stock.

Investments in quality go hand in hand with improvements in the skills of the workforce. Improved employee satisfaction, commitment and communication lead to an improved overall culture.

Additional research is needed to assess the evidence base in this area, but ASPE research aims to help practitioners and policy makers understand the range of social capital strategies that human services programs can use. This website contains links to materials prepared by ASPE when it led the effort to help the federal government understand how local, state and religious non-profit programs and organizations create and deploy "social capital" policies to increase employment, reduce poverty and improve the well-being of children and families and how local authorities can improve these efforts.

The main assumption of educational research is the idea that the education system is the main driver of change in society as a whole. For example, secondary education has been portrayed as an agent of economic development and most official documents confirm the existence of a correlation between the rising number of secondary school graduates and economic progress (Watson 1967).

Not surprisingly, research and policymaking developed streams that took into account how education as an important institution shaped overall development. This common paradigm of educational research and policy has been accompanied by studies on the universalization of compulsory education and the struggle to transform elite secondary education into a universal mass level.

## Is There A Moral Obligation To Invest In Human Capital?

The Business Roundtable, a consortium of 180 US CEOs who run some of the world's largest companies, has a new vision that puts corporate responsibility (CR) first, including investment in employees and supporting local communities. The new principals announced last summer represent business leaders' "commitment to promoting an economy that serves a broad electorate, including workers, members of local communities, local governments, suppliers, partners, members of the unions, creditors and others." Panelists stressed that increasing human capital should not be seen as a cost for investment ministers, but that HCP should serve as a toolkit for countries to make effective investments in their populations.

Whether all members believe it or not, the new policy set from the top is clearly defined by a moral obligation to invest in human capital. In this case, most members may have thought that this investment would also boost consumer spending and therefore their bottom lines. Still, the outcome of positive investment in human capital would be achieved with the framework set in the outlined principles.

Positive goodwill and a superior social agenda can lead to long-term economic and financial success. For example, a social agenda that includes market advantages for workers can attract the best workers and make a company's human capital more productive. Positive interactions with the community surrounding a facility or office can also lead to favorable bargaining power with local government officials and more profitable tax breaks and other contractual obligations.

I believe that companies that respect human dignity create and maintain a corporate culture in which employees, customers and suppliers are treated fairly, not as a means to an end but as people of intrinsic value, recognized and produced through safe products and services and safe jobs. Companies that respect fundamental rights will act in a way that supports and protects the individual rights of workers and customers, as well as of surrounding communities, and will avoid relationships that violate people's rights to health, education, security and a decent standard of living. Full engagement with all stakeholders, not just shareholders, will allow workers to personalise their work and life experiences.

Businesses can also be good citizens by supporting basic social institutions such as economies, education systems and working with a variety of governments and other organizations to protect the environment. In some industries, capturing human capital pays off for business operations and earnings, especially when it comes to employee satisfaction.

Satisfied employees work harder and are more productive, which affects customer loyalty.

At the organizational level, we found that HR departments that focus on workforce analytics to inform their employees of their decisions are the most effective - producing an average of $775,364 in revenue per employee. Ultimately, it should be left to companies to decide which measures they consider most important for organizational outcomes and which they consider least important. If your company is committed to investing in human data and acts on data-driven insights, you can choose which types of human analytics technology fits your needs the most.

The standard strategy for the distribution of labor considers human capital as a set of characteristics that contribute to employee productivity. It should be noted that contextual factors such as technology, trade unions, market conditions and business approaches are important and have a direct impact on costs, but linking alternative methods with HRM practices can increase the value of human capital with an enterprise value and expected returns. Reporting on human metrics requires more companies to discover value by tracking their employees as they count their pennies.

In corporate finance, human capital is one of the three main components of intellectual capital that together with tangible assets make up the total value of the company. Human capital encompasses how an organization uses its employees and resources to measure creativity and innovation. It is the value that workers and companies provide through the application of skills, knowledge and expertise.

Human capital is an intangible asset that is not listed on your company's balance sheet. Before you invest in your human capital and value it for your employees, you need to understand what it is.

Human capital is divided into three types:

1) knowledge capital

2) social capital

3) emotional capital

Creativity, flexibility and agility: these are personal intangible values that, for example, increase your value to your employer. Many theories rely on investing in human capital to the development of education and the role of human capital in economic development, productivity growth and innovation is often cited as justification for government subsidies to education and training. Preschool children, who are scolded for mastering grit in order to improve their college readiness, are an example of the logic of human capital.

If inequality is understood as a human capital deficit, eliminating inequality becomes not just a matter of wealth redistribution, but of human capital development (see, for example, its influence on popular vocational-education prescriptions as a cure for unemployment). The advantage of employers who see education, health care and human capital development as risks in the labour market is that nothing can be outsourced to workers. The pressure to find a passion for work is an example of the value language of human capital, and passion is another example of what Becker calls the "psychic income" - the gratuitous satisfaction of obtaining work that complements the unsatisfactory regular income.

They may be less concerned about moral obligation than about effectiveness in achieving results, and they make the task of leadership more difficult when asked to evaluate the moral dimension. Leaders in the emerging industries understand that ordinary workers in an organization are human beings, and that they have the same basic needs.

In addition to their effectiveness, they should be measured by the extent with which they create a corporate culture in which ethical principles are respected by people and never violated. In this case, an ethical corporate culture is defined as one in which all stakeholders are treated with due respect in an organization. Given the ethical focus, I believe that it can be argued that creating ethical corporate cultures is the most important role, job, and responsibility of a virtuous leader.

# Why Is Education The Most Important Element Of Human Capital?

Education is by far the most important element of human capital. Investing in education is the beginning of the rise from disadvantaged to opportunity abundance. To understand this, the following will follow the integration of human capital into the endogenous growth model, focusing on the two main areas of growth analysis promoted by Romer (1990) and Lucas (1988).

According to the 2001 OECD definition (2001) human capital in a nation consists of knowledge, skills and competences embodied in individual citizens which facilitate the formation of personal, social and economic well-being. Human capital is divided into three types: 1) knowledge capital, 2) social capital and 3) emotional capital. It measures the skills, education and skills attributed to work that affect their productivity and earning potential.

Many theories link investment in human capital to the development of education, and the role of human capital in economic development, productivity, growth and innovation is often cited as the reason for government subsidies to education and training. Workers' productivity is linked to their skills, education and qualifications. The idea that human skills and education are a source of capital that can be invested in the form of the nation as a whole when applied to the analysis of the nation has become a key element in understanding how businesses succeed in an era of innovation, where intellectual property is more important than factories and land to create value for businesses.

Gary Becker, Human Capital (1964)'s human capital is determined from Becker's point of view by education, training, medical treatment and the means of production. Human Capital Theory (HCT) has long been subordinated to the vaunted "knowledge-based economy" by the state education system and instrumentalized for economic growth.

Human capital theory has been accepted as the basis for educational policy decisions, planning and evaluation by many societies in the last fifty years. Human capital theory deals with economic growth and assumes that human labor should be treated as a commodity.

One of the principal problems in measuring human capital is the difficulty of measuring its quality, because it is not traded on the market like other commodities and is not assigned a clear market value. Taking into account the OECD definition (2001), it is difficult to find a way to measure the impact of human capital on the economy.

Neomarxist economists have argued that education does not lead to higher wages by increasing human capital, but by making workers more docile and dependable in the business environment. Human capital theory has experienced the same shortcomings and limitations when trying to explain these phenomena: its basic assumptions about human motives, goals, and decisions, it turns out, are not well founded. Modern critiques by sociologists and anthropologists argue against the theory of human capital, saying it offers simple principles that supposedly explain everyone's wages and time and that there is no universal connection between human capital and productivity or income.

The main assumption of educational research is the idea that the education system is the main driver of change in society as a whole. This has influenced educational researchers in their understanding of the quality of education, the adjustment of enrollment rates and the ability to perform the functions of education systems together with Durkheim's Human Capital Theory and his structural-functionalist approach to sociology. This common paradigm of educational research and policy goes hand in hand with the study of the universalization of compulsory education and the struggle to transform the upper-secondary elite into the mass on the general level.

In other words, society and researchers have placed trust in the transformative effects of education and its role in the promotion of development. Twenty years later, government officials and development partners meet regularly to reaffirm the importance of education for development and economic development, improve people's lives, and make education the goal.

Enrolment is rising promisingly worldwide, but learning levels remain low and many are lagging behind. For countries to benefit, they must unleash the potential of the human spirit. Growth, development and poverty reduction depend on people's knowledge and skills, not the number of years they spend in a classroom, so we need to shift our call for action from education to learning.

There are other factors that are also important for the development of human resources, and not only education is important for the development of these resources, it is values, knowledge and hard work. We can also see this in our families. Most of our mothers are not only educated, but they also control the whole family. They control their good values, they do what is best for others, and they behave just like their mothers. They know what to do. Thus, the knowledge of a mother leads to good control of the family. If education is ignored, it is impossible to govern a nation. Other factors are responsible for the growth of human resources and education is not only rooted in human development, but also in values, diligence and knowledge that lead to good results. Some of our mothers are not only educated, but also control the entire family.

# How To Understand The Analogy Between Human Capital And Physical Capital

Physical capital consists of man-made goods that support the production process. Human capital refers to the network of workers based on the general level of their influence in an industry. It includes a knowledge base of employees that measures the quality of the product.

Physical capital consists of inanimate assets such as cash, construction sites, equipment, real estate and inventory. Human and physical capital differ in ways that go beyond financial considerations. Human capital is by definition embedded in the nervous system of a particular individual and therefore does not belong to the individual, but to the living body itself.

As far as the mobility of human capital is concerned, it is not transnational; it is limited by nationality and culture. In societies that legalize slavery or at least enforce long-term transferable labor contracts, human capital itself cannot be bought or sold on the market because it is a temporary service that reflects the labor productivity of the individual to whom it belongs. Physical human capital is subject to depreciation for reasons other than the sense in which physical capital depreciates due to constant use.

On the other hand, human capital is declining due to age, a factor largely reduced by investment in health and education. This type of investment costs arise because investors expect to gain additional benefits over a longer period in the future. Another difference is goodwill, which is one of the largest components of goodwill in human capital.

Indeed, goodwill is one of the few places where analysts can find the value of human capital on a balance sheet. Your human capital consists of everything you learned at school, everything you learned during your family education that taught you values such as arriving on time for work, finishing what you started, what you learned at work, the education you received, how you learned most of your singing voice and sprinting skills and everything you read and think about what you want to do in life, what you have not yet put into practice. Physical capital is easily found and noted on balance sheets, but the value for human capital is much more difficult to assume.

Your human capital includes your unique genetic predispositions and talents that make you unique, as well as the unique way in which your brain and body have evolved and learned to adapt to events throughout your life. There is a significant difference between human capital and physical capital, but both are crucial for a successful construction company. We hope this article has helped you understand the difference between the two types of capital.

Effective construction and resource management plans must take into account both human and physical capital. A new assessment of human capital for 157 countries follows a similar measurement by the Institute for Health Metrics and Evaluation (IHME) for 195 countries that was published in September in the medical journal The Lancet. The new metric combines five indicators of health and education, including the likelihood of dying between the ages of five and 15, the 60% likelihood of stunted growth in the education years that the average child will complete before the age of 18 and the score that the average child is likely to achieve on school tests to measure how much human capital is likely to accumulate a person born today.

A higher average education level, ceteris paribus, is intended to reduce inequality of income by enabling a larger proportion of the population to benefit from activities with higher qualifications, as the results of Sylwester (2003) for OECD countries in an extended country sample for the 1970-1990 period show. There is agreement on the existence of a positive economic return to education in terms of income levels, but theoretical predictions of inequality due to the impact of changes in enrollment are not straightforward.

As someone with the skills and knowledge of old ideas, this article argues that in the recent history of HC and its rehabilitation additional variables that explain economic growth have not been taken into consideration in conventional macroeconomic analysis. Section 2 briefly presents two main methods that can be used to measure the value of HBC from an aggregate perspective to understand the contribution of that value to the total wealth of a nation.

By investing themselves, people increase the choices available to them. Section 3 addresses approaches based on private and individual investment decisions made by the Chicago Human Capital School, Schultz and Becker and the resulting literature aimed to measure the total and differential stock of individuals based on different characteristics of the amount of HC in individuals and determine their source. For Smith, this includes the acquired and useful skills of residents and members of society, as well as the idea of capital.

## The Role Of Human Capital In The Analogy Of The Firm

I would argue that if a person possesses the skills and knowledge of old ideas, the recent history of HC and its rehabilitation are additional variables that help explain economic growth that cannot be explained by conventional macroeconomic analysis.

Human capital refers to the acquired skills and talents a person has acquired to increase their success in life. Your Human Capital consists of everything you learned at school, everything you learned during your family adoption, which taught you values of great importance as arriving on time for work, finishing what you started, what you learned at work, the education you received, how you learned most of your singing voice and sprinting skills and everything you read and think about what you want to do in life and what you have not yet put into practice. This includes your unique genetic predispositions and talents that make you special, and the unique way in which your brain and body have evolved and learned to adapt to circumstances throughout your life.

Let me begin by presenting the concept of human capital as an intangible asset, as applied to financial theory. Human capital is defined as the present value of your projected labor income during your working years. This is the question you need to answer if you want to use this asset to diversify and build your wealth.

The economic value of an employee's experience and skills includes assets such as education, training, intelligence, skills, health and other things that employers value, such as loyalty and punctuality. Human capital, of course, cannot be bought and sold for free like a man, since there are no slaves or material forms of capital, but its producers and services can be employed at a price of wages. They can be strengthened by investments that improve their income prospects.

The wage effect lowers the wage premium because the supply of skilled workers increases rather than decreases the inequality (for a discussion see Bergh and Fink, 2008; De Gregorio and Lee, 2002 ). An important point about education and inequality is that the relationship is monotonous rather than linear, and the educational effect is unevenly distributed rather than balanced (for an analogy to the Kuznets process, see Rehme, 2007).

None of the studies examined here suggests a positive correlation between inequality and the unequal effect of education on income and income inequality, and the majority of these studies balance each other out. In many of these studies, educational variables (e.g. Proportion of secondary and tertiary education and average school years) are introduced as control variables to measure the development of human capital.

Human capital is an intangible asset that is not listed on a company's balance sheet but which includes things like employee experience and skills. Because work is not considered equivalent, employers can improve human capital by investing in education and training that benefits their employees. For example, if Company X invests $2 million in human capital and generates a total return of $1.5 million, managers can compare year after year the ROI of their human capital to track the return and improve its relationship to human capital investment.

When it is time to let inferior performers go, this is a task that must be performed with dignity and respect, with the precision of a surgeon who cuts to heal. In today's highly competitive talent market, we are trying to inspire human capital investors to take responsibility so that their strengths can be exploited to the full. Businesses need good people, which means they need to understand what they are good at.

There is a universal need for workers to do meaningful work, to be in communion with others and to make a difference in the world. Humans are not assets, inventories, or resources; they are individuals who have a right to a purpose in their lives, to assemble in an organization and, above all, to do something for the lives of others.

People analytics is an essential part of running a powerful company, but there is nothing better to think about than people analytics. You don't need data to know that loyal and satisfied employees are those who have the opportunity to grow because they are in line with the growing growth of the company.

The distortion in the measurement of the labour force and the treatment of the public expenditure on education and medical care can be corrected by utilizing the concept of human capital. The important unresolved question of whether economic growth is changing the pattern of wages, salaries, and personal income distribution can be resolved by taking investment in human capital into account. Apart from the fact that the esteemed producer of goods misses out on many improvements, he is still a good part of capital.

Throughout your career, you convert human capital into financial capital by saving and investing a portion of your work income. Assuming that you save and invest by increasing your working income, your financial capital will increase. In contrast, it will be lower at this stage because you have had no chance to save or invest.

The only person who can invest in human capital with complete confidence that his fruits will not be withheld in future remuneration is the individual. When investments are made by other companies, individuals have less incentive to invest resources in their own way, especially if it is a cheaper way to increase productivity. If an employee decides to quit his job and is offered a higher salary in a competing company in the same sector, the investment that the employer has made in the past to improve the employee's professional skills is lost by the employer the last time the employee steps outside.

## Trends In Human Capital In North America

At the board level, companies attach great importance to analytics to make decisions about how to nurture talent, find ways to retain talent, and use talent recruitment methods. Board statutes are being expanded, many companies focus on human capital and an increasing number of organizations are using quantitative analysis to measure their efforts including strategic risks and rewards. Conscious business models in the form of social entrepreneurship, conscious capitalism, B Corp certification, benefit corporate certification and fair trade certification are increasingly recognized and well received by customers and the public.

When it comes to human resources, the metrics include measures such as employee retention, reduction of sick leave, and employee engagement. In addition to assessing hard skills such as standards, soft skills such as communication, companies are also looking for candidates who are motivated by the company's mission and values. In the human capital market, candidates are looking to see whether a company offers them a core value system that is dovetailed with their own.

How companies adapt to a more remote and digital work environment will play an important role in influencing the next trends of the coming decades. By understanding the human capital trends that shape human capital, organizations can increase productivity, reduce turnover, and ultimately generate more profits. In the coming year, seeing changes in workers' requirements, technology and business environment and positioning ourselves to take advantage of them, will work well for all of us.

Human resources organizations exist in an organizational environment that is as turbulent and competitive as the environment in which companies find themselves. The changing nature of manpower, global competition, advancements in information technology and new knowledge, the uneven recovery from the 2008 global recession, demand for sustainable organizational performance and a host of other changes are forcing organizations to review and re-examine how they operate. Organizations are using new technologies to change their structure, redesign their work, relocate their workforce and improve work processes in order to respond to the increasingly demanding and unpredictable global competitive environment (Lawler and Worley, 2011).

Human capital management is the process of managing workers to improve the overall performance of an organization. Its main functions are the management of employee profiles, payrolls, remuneration, benefits, perks, recruitment and selection, training and development, and workforce analysis. An essential driver of an organizational and performance approach is its business strategy.

The term human capital describes people, organisations, whole countries and other geographical areas. It refers to the collective value of knowledge, skills, creativity and other factors in a group of people who are doing work. Human capital does not define the value of people but seeks to define and maximize the economic value of employees "qualifications and experience".

According to a survey, about 60 percent of workers want to work full-time during the COVID-19 pandemic. An alternative labour force, including the so-called "gig economy," is seen as the only way for people to make their working hours more flexible by paying for tasks with contracted hours. Companies are considering paying contractors for contracts through contractor websites such as Fiverr and Upwork.

Technology adoption and take-up will be a priority for companies aiming to unify and distribute the workforce that first works digitally. Ensuring that employees have the skills they need is a top priority for business leaders. The increasing popularity of big data in the HR function creates opportunities for companies operating in the human resources software market to gain a stronger customer base and offer advanced solutions.

The increasing demand for streamlining human resources activities, rearing and growing technological progress, which shortens periods of time and contributes to a fast and easy flow of activities, as well as the increased adoption of digital human resources technologies are some of the many factors expected to accelerate the expansion of the global human capital management market. Growing demand for unified HCM portals for employee activities, transparent visibility of the company's activities, employee presence and leave, perks and benefits, payroll, remuneration, personnel rules and procedures and estimates also support the HR software market.

According to a study by KPMG, 77% of CEOs surveyed are building their use of collaboration and communication tools, and 67% are likely to invest in technology compared to 33% investing in their employees' "skills. The global human capital trends report from Deloitte 2021 found that adoption of digital collaboration platforms is the most important factor in maintaining this new way of working. Research by renowned HR thinker and analyst Josh Bersin takes this concept to another level.

In preparation for the reboot in the post coronavirus world, Gartner has identified two technology classes for this year's HCM trends that will better support HR managers. Flexible workplaces and the rapid move from home to work have made companies curious to see how employee productivity develops.

Future Workplace Views surveyed 1,501 workers across North America to find out which wellness perks are most important to them and how these perks affect productivity. Almost half of the workers we surveyed said that poor air quality made their day more difficult, and more than a third said they lost hours of productivity as a result.

In carrying out this research, I recommend that HR managers working with property and facility managers take a holistic view of their work environment, including the definition of well-being at work (physical well-being, emotional well-being and environmental well-being) and carry out an audit to identify how all aspects of the work environment can be improved. Based on competitive intelligence and benchmarking, our research reports that the HCM (Human Capital Management) solutions on the market are designed to provide entry level support, customer profile, M&A and launch support.

# Contemporary Policy Issues Surrounding Human Capital

Human resources experts have come a long way, from the processing of employee papers to strategic positions with an executive chair at the management table. The corporate landscape is changing with increasing speed, as is the role of personnel managers. Having established a platform for completing qualifications and assessing the suitability of candidates, I have seen that adequate insights into the skills and behaviours of candidates provide HR teams with valuable information to help address the most pressing human resources challenges.

The federal workforce plays a critical role in carrying out the important mission of federal agencies serving the American people. But Federal agencies are facing a number of management challenges owing to fiscal constraints, demographic changes, a wave of Federal Retirements and the changing role of the public sector. Leading practices in human capital management can help federal agencies to face a number of challenges.

Human resources departments work differently today than they did a decade ago. Changes in the labour market, regulatory requirements and compliance issues have forced HR managers to become fast partners in the strategic development of companies. Topics such as cash flow, competition and revenue growth are top priorities for small entrepreneurs and their teams.

Small business owners need to understand the challenges they face to be better prepared to address staffing issues as their workforce grows. HR agencies must develop the ability to identify basic skills and career leaders, and rely on individual performance metrics and feedback from superiors and employees to understand skill development needs.

While mega-companies like Amazon invest hundreds of millions of dollars in labor-development initiatives, many companies are reluctant to invest in education and development. Implementing innovative approaches to learning new skills such as self-directed online learning, on-the-job coaching and virtual training can help improve employee engagement and reduce costly turnover. The development of skills and the realignment of HR specialists into business partners and strategic consultants should also be on the list.

Education and development should not swallow up a large part of a company's budget. Creating a system that rewards employees for excellence is one way to offset a lower salary. Large systems for talent work differ from systems that challenge HR managers.

With good talent no longer available for internal positions, HR managers need to find ways to conclude long-term contracts and develop other suitable talent. In contrast, HR 3.0 offices focus on building and maintaining positive work experiences so that employees perform at their best. Human resources specialists work closely with superiors and business partners to create high-performing organizations.

New practices and systems related to manpower management will be developed with the involvement of superiors. Expanding workforce analysis to include personal preferences, goals, and decisions will enable companies to be proactive in creating desirable employee experiences and strategically engage their workforce rather than remain reactive.

Equipped with these insights, HR is better equipped to take a leading position as a consultant and manager when it comes to encouraging its organizations to make positive changes. HR experts at the Society for Human Resource Management (SHRM) say in a survey today that employee engagement, the development of the next generation of leaders or competitive remuneration and retention matters. HR assessments confirm what C-suite executives from other disciplines said in an accompanying survey that their biggest challenge is to retain their highly-performing employees and maintain competitive advantages through employee retention, underscoring the importance of HRs role in maintaining competitiveness in today's business environment.

To achieve this goal, motivate your management team and give them the chance to develop their skills. Leadership development is crucial to keep them engaged, motivated and prepared so that they can assume more responsibility in the future. Investments in training and development of lower-level staff are a frequent personnel problem.

These factors indicate that the process of developing and implementing Human Resources policy in the Health sector is an ongoing adjustment process, not only due to the need for population change and staffing expectations, but also because it is carried out without the full participation of the staff. HRH policy reforms are attempts to expand health care without foreseeing the long-term impact of major trends such as population aging, likely demand for services, and labor demand. The impact of reforms in the HRH should be considered in retrospect if (a) the proposed plans are found to be infeasible due to prohibitive staffing costs, (b) the plans are rejected by professional groups, (c) they have an unrealistic view of the initial situation and (d) they require changes from organisations that are already working with difficult views on the current organisational capacity and political acceptance for changes in these organisations.

If inequality is understood from the point of view of the human capital deficit, eliminating inequality becomes not only a matter of wealth redistribution, but also of the development of human capital (see, for example, its influence on popular recipes for vocational training as a cure for unemployment). It is beneficial for employers to treat education, health care and human capital development as risks in the labour market, rather than outsourcing them to workers.

## How Canada Views Human Capital

In a knowledge-based economy, it is the quality of human capital that distinguishes high-performing cities and regions. Cities not only compete for business and foreign investment, but also try to attract well-educated, skilled and mobile workers based on the facilities and quality of life they offer to their communities. Simply put, our cities have a healthy, educated, and diverse workforce.

Based on the Human Capital Index, which measures variables such as unemployment, labor-force participation rates, workers health and well-being and skill levels, the regions of Calgary, Toronto and Vancouver in Canada finished ahead of Seattle, New York, Los Angeles and Chicago in the North America rankings. The demand for highly skilled talent in Asia is growing with rapid technological development, the growth of high-tech sectors and an aging population, according to the Pacific Foundation of Canada. In Asia, a young, well-educated workforce and leaders in research and innovation offer Canada hopeful opportunities.

Faced with the challenges of globalization, Canada has made the most of its internal globalization and its competitive advantage over a multicultural population. Canada has one of the highest net immigration rates in the world and receives more immigrants per capita than Europe, Britain and the United States.

This trend is likely to remain for the foreseeable future an integral part of Canadian immigration policy and demography, as the focus on human capital and immigration is increasingly woven into economic policy.

The human capital model of immigration assumes that the selection of immigrants with high human capital is beneficial in the long term. The problem of shortages of physical capital and labor surpluses in countries can be solved by accelerating the formation of human capital through private and public investments in education and health sectors and through surpluses in their economies. Human resources can be transformed into human capital through effective use of education, health, and moral values.

Global companies focus on developing and acquiring talent to strengthen their competitiveness, promote sustainable growth, manage risks, and develop innovative products and services. Indeed, the ability to attract, develop, and retain leadership talent has become an important factor in capital investment, corporate strategy, and organizational growth. Recent US research shows that geographical regions that invest in human capital and the economic progress of immigrants living in their countries help boost their long- and short-term economic growth.

Since the points system was introduced in 1967, Canada has sought to target immigration specifically at potential immigrants whose characteristics match Canada's evolving needs and interests. Canada's points system, used in the 1990 "s and early 2000" s to select economic migrants, was based on a human-capital model of immigration. This model, for example, takes a broad, long-term view of desirable characteristics of human capital, and the selection model is based on the need to address the shortage of manpower and skills.

Immigrant selection under the federal worker program (FSWP) continues to be based on the human capital model of immigration but other immigration selection programs have been introduced that focus on short-term labor market needs, not on skill shortages. This shift in focus is aimed at improving the labour market outcomes of immigrants entering the labour market.

Canada began to adopt policies to manage immigration at the end of the nineteenth century. From 1962, regulatory changes were introduced to overturn the racial dimensions of Canadian immigration policy.

In 1971, Premier Pierre Elliott Trudeau announced that Canada would have two official languages and that the official culture of each ethnic group would take precedence over the other. Unlike the U.S. "melting pot" approach to diversity in the United

States [3], Canadian multiculturalism implies harmonious coexistence of different cultures, ethnicities and languages and the strengthening of ethnic minorities.

Economic theorists and social scientists who have studied Canada's economic and immigration policies suggest that Canada has a long history of identity building in which it has exploited ethnic labor and maintained a moderate level of the negation and subjugation of minorities. This paper provides estimates of the market-based human capital stock in Canada for the 1970-2007 period based on a lifelong income approach and compares it to the physical and natural capital stocks.

The methodology used for this chapter was a labour-based measurement of Canada's human capital resources from 1971 through 1996 based on completion of education and number of years of work experience aimed to measure differences in the quality of training and the market relevance of various types of training for work experience. Unlike measures of human capital, which are based on average school years, the approach to labor income does not assume that differences in productivity between workers are proportional to differences in educational attainment.

## How Europe Views Human Capital

I'd like to cover a bit of the typology of human capital development in EU countries. The study focuses on long-term economic and social trends in Central and Eastern Europe countries and outlines a number of factors that threaten economic performance of new members, including unfavourable demographic trends, under exploitation of human capital, brain migration and insufficient investment in education and skills. It also outlines an expansion of the Human Capital Index to address specific challenges in education, health, and well-being facing countries in Europe and Central Asia.

This underscores the basic theoretical concepts of human capital and its quantitative measurements. It also shows that in the past, regional disparities between European regions as a whole can be regarded as an important factor causing these disparities. Additionally, the relationship between historical human capital and current economic results is highlighted to illustrate the importance for human capital in general and for a long-term view of economic policy in particular.

The public sector is responsible for investing in human capital, while the private sector uses it to create, strengthen and develop physical capital. On average, the public investment in human capital is three times higher than public investment in physical capital.

We need an education system that turns lifelong learners into innovators. The education system of the future will be very different from that in many countries today. For future prosperity we must provide a system of quality education, from early childhood, so that we have a skilled and innovative population who can meet the new challenges and opportunities of the 21st century.

In relation to the quantitative aspect of human capital investment covered, this ignores the importance of the quality aspect of human capital. This is one reason why it has made graduation rates one of its five headline targets.

Many developing countries face similar educational, economic, and political choices that European countries make in their phases of economic development. Our focus is not only on formal school systems, but also with early childhood development, vocational training, the importance of university education in a knowledge-based economy, the ongoing training of staff and the growing importance of lifelong learning.

For these reasons, the long-term view of the European region points to potential obstacles to the formation of human capital in developing countries. The greatest regional disparities in the formation of human capital are found in Europe.

The main pull factors are better career opportunities and remuneration, while corruption, social inequality, educational opportunities, and racial inequality, such as government "bumiputera" (affirmative action) policies, are among the main drivers. In addition to human migration, the social environment is also considered to be a major reason for population shifts. For example, Lithuania lost over 100,000 citizens in 2003, many of them young and well educated, mainly due to emigration to Ireland.

Most people moving within the EU are highly qualified: 80% of people who have moved to another EU Member State in the last ten years have a medium to high level of education. Many rural communities in the Appalachian Mountains in the United States are experiencing a "brain drain," as young college students migrate for professional and political reasons to the region's urban areas, where they are offered opportunities that rural communities cannot.

Japan has a similar program that has done well but was largely focused on urbanisation of rural areas of the country and bringing them into a less agrarian lifestyle. The program has been increasingly successful in attracting donations since its launch in 2008, especially under Prime Minister Shinzo Abe's administration, as part of his regional revival initiative, which doubled the cap on tax-deductible donations. The results show a positive link between dependent and independent variables and confirm that the digitalisation of the economy and the development of human capital can lead to greater prosperity for the population.

It aims to support human capital in the early stages of local investment, which is crucial to help certain countries in the region offset their investment efforts in the region. The program means that foreign-born and foreign-trained workers can decide to return part of their income tax to their home country to support the formation of human capital. In Japan, this can be used as a tax credit on their tax bill the following year.

# How The United States Invests In Human Capital

To maximize these benefits and ensure that the United States does not lose a step, it would be wise for politics and business to focus on America's human capital. Human capital is defined as the stock of knowledge, skills and other personal qualities that embody people who help them to be productive. It encompasses skills, education, talents, habits, and personal networks that enable individuals to generate income.

In companies, this is called talent management or human resources departments. Investment in so-called human capital workers cannot be separated from the ability and quality of work that affects productivity, such as education. Anyone who aspires to formal education, from early childhood through the formal school system to adult education programmes and informal learning in the workplace and work experience, represents an investment in human capital.

Investments in human capital, including expenditures in higher education, staff training, leadership development, performance management systems, employee morale and retention programs and other organizational development measures, help create and nurture a skilled, skilled, motivated and productive workforce. There are several compelling economic and entrepreneurial reasons to invest in human capital. Human capital influences economic growth by contributing to the development of the economy by increasing people's knowledge and skills.

Consumer spending and business investment not only boost economic growth, but also play a prominent role in determining workers' "education and development. The knowledge and skills of its people provide economic value, and skilled labor leads to higher productivity. The process of training the workforce is the kind of investment that is a capital investment, such as an investment in equipment in human capital.

The labour force system has not exhausted its potential to help adult workers build up their human capital. It is time for the workforce to take its place in preschools, kindergartens, elementary schools, secondary schools, and traditional four-year colleges and institutions to promote education and develop the human capital of our lives.

Hybrid programmes for adult workers should be introduced into the labour force system. Our adult workforce includes 80-90 million full-time workers who lack enough skills, human capital and personal interests to pursue a bachelor's degree. Many of these workers would benefit from high-quality hybrid labor-force programs that combine the pedagogical rigor of postsecondary education with the flexibility of labor-market-oriented labor-force training.

Improving your employees offers opportunities for growth and learning and also improves your profits. When individuals, companies, and organizations perform better, they contribute to the success of the economy as a whole.

Nobel prize-winning economist Gary Becker explained the relationship between human capital and economic growth when he wrote: "Economic growth depends on the synergy between new knowledge and human capital and when large gains in education and training are accompanied by large advances in technological knowledge, countries can achieve considerable economic growth".

Our work in these countries emphasises the efficiency and quality of policy reforms and the mobilisation of national resources so that they do not spend more than is spent. An example of this approach is our country's commitment to Madagascar, which invests in human capital under the Development Policy and Operations series.

Human capital consists of knowledge, skills and health that people invest and accumulate throughout their lives to fulfill their potential as productive members of society. Investment in nutrition, health care, quality education and professional skills contributes to human capital development and is the key to ending extreme poverty and creating a more inclusive society. Protecting people and investing in them is one of the three main ways the United States is working to achieve our goal of ending extreme poverty by 2030 and increasing shared prosperity in all countries.

Human capital contributes significantly to productivity, as workers with higher education and skills tend to produce more. People invest in human capital for reasons similar to those of corporations in physical capital and individuals in financial assets when they hope to generate income.

They can increase income, improve health, and improve a person's lifestyle for long stretches of their life. Recent research suggests that the increase in human capital accounts for about 20% of US productivity growth between 1950 and 2007. But productivity growth slowed to 0.4% from 2011 to 20156 from 2.5% per year from 1995 to 2010. This worries economists, as productivity is a key factor in economic growth and real wages and living standards.

## How Has Covid-19 Changed Investment In Human Capital?

Production potential is described in terms of the endowment of the economy – labour and physical capital, including infrastructure, intangible assets, human capital, natural capital and a diversified stock of technical knowledge. This endowment determines the overall level of economic productivity, which in turn largely determines a country's material standard of living. Based on a meritocracy and income-based approach, the Office of National Statistics measures the available stock of human capital for the working-age population in monetary terms by subtracting life incomes.

The main message from that data is that the public sector still plays a leading role in the sourcing of human capital in the economy. Public investments in human capital are four times higher than investment in human capital in the private sector. On average, public investment in human capital is three times higher than public investment in physical capital.

The current definition of investment should be extended to investment in human capital. The public sector should be responsible for the investment in human capital, while the private sector should use human capital to create value, strengthen it and develop physical capital. Both private and public investment should be targeted to create the conditions for sustainable productivity growth.

For example, there are several persistent gaps in investment that could be closed, including infrastructure, affordable housing and green technologies. Additional government investment in basic research and R&D to return to the levels of the last decade could also help.

Organizations are likely to seek in the future for meaningful ways to measure culture and to show progress. A renewed debate could lead to a more unified approach to investment in human capital that must be followed by fundamental and necessary changes in the national statistical systems and national accounts.

The coronavirus crisis is a human crisis that requires human-centered measurements and solutions. Research and current discussions in our Human Capital Investment Reporting Council (HC IRC) suggest an increased focus on human capital reporting, transparency and disclosure is an important basis for stakeholder action in the community. Investing in and prioritising six areas related to human capital can help organisations mitigate the risks and negative impacts of COVID-19.

Investors and regulators, in turn, are looking for boards to strengthen their governance of human capital. Companies that create a framework for managing human capital are seen as better investments and better equipped to create long-term value, and regulators such as the US Securities and Exchange Commission are urging companies to disclose the measures they take to protect their employees' health in upcoming earnings releases. This change took place during the COVID 19 crisis, as employees increasingly see the Board of Directors as a key stakeholder in the economic recovery.

Companies that responded to the recent unprecedented bull market by strengthening their balance sheets, investing in innovation, and caring for their employees have proven resilient to the ongoing crisis. The recent performance of stakeholder-oriented companies, which builds on a long history of outperformance of companies that are high on a variety of ESG (ecological, social and governance) criteria, stems from a new era of focus on sustainable community investment (s) around issues such as climate change.

Although COVID-19 has shed new light on social issues, the importance of human capital for the success of a company is no secret. Recent market volatility has shown that investors are uncertain about many things, including labor risk and whether investors can trust future organizational responses. Much of the industry has gone beyond platitudes such as "our most valuable asset is people" and has introduced a thoughtful measurement and assessment of return on investment in human capital management (HCM).

The Shareholder Value Age has etched disturbing ideas and practices into our management and operating habits, which we must destroy if we are to succeed in the new era of human capital. To enter this new era, we must continue on the path of transformation, which focuses on people, not technology. Rapid transformation and forced experiments with distance learning and work are not ideal, but they offer a way into the new era.

Telepresence, health care, distance learning and distance work will remain. Rapid adaptation works best when we are doing it while we are doing it, not when we are away from it.

Behavioural changes, such as greater adoption of technology, strengthen production potential. Negative effects, on the other hand, result from increasing protectionist attitudes and prolonged uncertainty and scarring.

The concept of economic rent (Berk and van Binsbergen 2015) defines the added value of a fund as a function of the gross alpha or the size of assets under management. Knowledge and skills from investments in human capital contribute to Value Added (VA), and in the case of investment funds, this is reflected in better performance. Labour productivity (GDP in volumes divided by hours worked) and its influence on multifactor productivity (also known as total factor productivity) and capital deepening (more capital per employee).

The World Bank Human Capital Index for Groups 2020 includes data on health and education from 174 countries, covering 98 percent of the population in the world (through March 2020) to provide a baseline for children's health and education before the pandemic. The index provides a decade-long overview of human capital performance from 2010 to 2020 and identifies improvements in all regions for which data is available, regardless of income level. These gains are largely due to improvements in health care, reflected in better survival rates for children and adults, lower stunting, and higher enrollment.

Also known as Human Capital.

# What Is The State Of Human Capital In The World Today?

A child born today in MENA is expected to achieve an average of 57% of its future productivity. A country score of 0.70 on the Human Capital Index is a score that indicates the future earning potential of a child born today, or 70 if he or she has completed an education and is in full health.

The Human Capital Report assesses how countries develop and use their human capital, with a focus on learning and employment. Like the Index, the report will be a tool for companies, governments, and others to evaluate the global pool of talent and design interventions. The 215 report covers 124 countries, representing 92% of the world's population and 98% of the global GDP. It also contains a lot about what the world is doing to build and use its human capital.

The World Bank's clients and donors are participating in human capital projects in part of an accelerated global effort to transform human capital outcomes. Human capital is a domain of development data and the World Bank Group works with member nations to build capacity and improve data quality. Starting in October 2020, the HCI Country Briefs will include a number of selected complementary indicators to present HCI from a broader regional and country-specific perspective of human capital.

Lebanon and Oman, which have lower per capita incomes and higher living standards than other countries, struggle with differences in access to high-quality education opportunities for parts of their population. Protecting and investing in people is crucial as countries work to lay the foundations for sustainable and inclusive recovery and future growth. The participation complements the World Bank Group's long-standing engagement with countries and sectors that contribute to human development.

In order to bring together these different dimensions of human capital into a single whole we have combined them in the World Bank Group into a single index measuring the impact of a lack of investment in human capital in terms of the loss of productivity for the next generation of workers. Using four case studies, researchers identified the most pressing human capital problems in many countries, compiled strategies and approaches to address them, examined the availability of resources and assessed the strategies put in place. They interviewed knowledgeable government and private sector officials in each country, analysed public reports and various secondary data sources (e.g. Population, education and labour market data at country level, government organisations and international databases).

In the latest edition of the annual human capital index of the World Bank, which measures the key components of human capital in the countries, India ranks 116th. It rose from 0.49 to 0.44 in 2018, according to the World Bank's Human Capital Index report released on Wednesday. The report includes health and education data from 174 countries that by March 2020 will cover 98% of the global population. It provides a baseline for health and education for children before the pandemic, with the lowest-income countries making the most progress.

The World Bank's Human Capital Index encourages countries to invest urgently in human capital. Human Capital is an intangible asset which is not listed on a company's balance sheet but includes things like employee experience and skills. The economic value of workers' experience and skills include assets such as education, training, intelligence, skills, health and other things that employers value, such as loyalty and punctuality.

In a technology-driven economy, intangible assets such as software products are less pure than brain power. Employers can improve the quality of human capital by investing in training, experience and skill of employees, regardless of their economic value to the employer or the economy as a whole. In companies, they are called talent management or human resources.

The top 5 countries on this index are Finland, Norway, Switzerland, Canada, and Japan, which are doing the best to maximize HCI. Not surprisingly, MENA's HCI ranges from 0.67 in the United Arab

Emirates (UAE) to 0.37 in Yemen. Conflict-affected countries such as Iraq and Yemen have the lowest HCI indices, raising important questions about how to support the protection and improvement of human capital in the midst of conflict.

Today, it seems the countries investing the most in people to improve education, access to basic services, and quality of life are improving Human Capital outcomes the best.

## The Role Of Human Capital In The Industrial Era

In some cases, human capital is seen as a fundamental factor of economic prosperity (see Hippe 2014). The OECD has proposed a more comprehensive approach to human capital. OECD more focuses on its economic dimension and defines human capital as knowledge, skills, competences and other attributes of persons relevant to economic activity (OECD, 1998).

Educational activities are considered the most important investment products of human capital (Didenko, 2013). The development of long-term trends in private efficiency and human capital in the industrial past (Dodenko 2013) was made possible by the use of the Kuznet curve. The theory of economic growth differs from the method of natural cost in assessing the endogeno genicity and exogenousity of human capital, but it still regards human capital as a key indicator of socioeconomic development.

Human capital acted as a catalyst to increase the productivity of the smart manufacturing industry of the 1940s. The success or failure of the industry depended on human capital contributing in its own way to its success and productivity. The industry could not have survived without human capital, the skills, knowledge, and ability to translate concepts from abstract thinking into reality and create added value for the organization.

Abstract This research highlights the role of human capital in modern economic development. In the context of the Fourth Industrial Revolution, high-quality human capital, created by innovation, has become a key factor in building the competitiveness of individual companies and the economy as a whole. The digital transformation of public life has also had a significant impact on the development of human capital.

Human capital is a key factor for economic development and a key element for future growth (Hippe, 2013; Hanushek and Woessmann, 2015). At the regional level, the need is even more evident, as human capital is paramount in addressing regional disparities in development (Gennaioli et al. However, the historical role of human capital formation is still not well understood.

Major regional differences characterise the formation of human capital in Europe. Human capital is divided into three types: 1) knowledge capital, 2) social capital and 3) emotional capital. It measures health, quality of education and standard of living.

With these two definitions above we can see that experience, knowledge, skills, and education are critical to an organization's human capital, which essentially underscores the importance of human capital in smart manufacturing in the industry 4.0 revolution. As a result, the production of human capital that can benefit from this revolution is necessary for the competitiveness of smart manufacturing. Many theories link investment in human capital development and education to the role human capital plays in economic development, productivity growth, and innovation, and are often cited as justification for government subsidies for education and training.

The problem of the shortages of physical capital and labour surpluses in countries can be solved by accelerating the formation of human capital through private and public investments in the education and health sectors as well as surpluses in their economies. Human resources can be transformed into human capital through effective inputs such as education, health, and moral values. The transformation of human resources into productive human resources through these inputs is the process of human capital formation.

Donald Street describes the Spanish origins of human capital theory and highlights Gaspar Melchor de Jovellanos, an eighteenth-century Spanish economist whose ancestors dealt with education, health and migration in modern human capital theories as well as the three major types of investment in human capital (Street 1988). This column shows that, despite the continuing impact of mechanization on textile and iron production and the economic expansion on the eve of the Industrial Revolution, mills and skilled carpenters have specialized in the construction and repair of water mills. Human capital remains a key factor in economic growth, despite the preoccupation with industrial and post-industrial knowledge and information cycles in economic development.

The persistent concerns of policymakers about the supply of qualified personnel that is needed to keep up with technological change stem from the idea that technological progress and catching up depend on availability of human capital. Although economic historians discuss the role of human capital in the British Industrial Revolution, it is agreed that the British leadership of the industrial revolution owed little to the educational system and that literacy rates in England were mediocre compared to other European countries (Mitch 1992, 1999 ). Recent work on human capital suggests that we should reconsider this consensus (Mokyr 2009).

## The Role Of Human Capital In The Information Age

These recent developments reflect a clear and growing market appetite to understand how companies manage and measure human capital. Many influential groups identify human capital as key to long-term value. Human resources in the information age have become human resources that know how to access and use all kinds of information to enhance their creativity.

Digital technologies are forcing companies across industries to rethink how they communicate with customers and develop products and services that serve their needs. As the focus on human capital and corporate governance increases, more and more stakeholders, led by large institutional investors, are trying to understand how companies integrate human capital considerations into overarching strategies for creating long-term value.

The introduction of the information and communication technology (ICT) has played an important role in almost all aspects of modern society. It affects daily life and macroeconomic growth, which in turn affects society by improving infrastructure and living standards. The information age is made possible by technologies developed during the digital revolution, which in turn was based on the development of the technological revolution.

The information age, also known as the digital age, the digital age or the new media age, is a historic period that began in the mid-twentieth century and is characterized by a rapid and unprecedented transition from the traditional industry established by the Industrial Revolution to an information technology-based economy. It was argued that the information age was an essential part of capitalism. The beginning of the information age is connected with the development of transistor technology.

According to the United Nations Public Administration Network, the information age was created to capitalize on the advances of computer microminiaturization, which led to a modernized information and communication process with wider usage in society and became a driving force in social evolution. In the information age, managed primarily by newspapers, radio, and television, information was primary.

Analysis of the prospects of information age technologies in the context of development. The purpose of this sectoral study is to help Member States make decisions that are consistent with national needs and other sectoral economic plans. It is important to examine the volume of investment, the possible sources of financing, the financing conditions and the general economic aspects of the construction of the information age industry.

Human capital is thought to be related to economic growth, productivity, and profitability. Investments in human capital, including expenditures on higher education, staff training, leadership development, performance management systems, employee morale and retention programs and other organizational development measures, help create and nurture a skilled, skilled, motivated and productive workforce. However, many businesses, especially small businesses, do not realise that continuous investment in human capital enables companies to adapt, grow and remain competitive.

Goode (1959) defined human capital as knowledge, skills, attitudes, talents and other acquired qualities that contribute to the production of particular work that leads to economic value. As people come with diverse skills and knowledge, human capital can help boost an economy. Like other assets, however, it can lose value due to long bouts of unemployment and inability to keep pace with technology and innovation.

The framework of Marxist epistemology is used in this article to understand the dialectical relationship between capital, digital labour and labour in the current information age. In this respect, Marxism is valid and decisive as an epistemological tool that helps students of the social sciences, labor relations and personnel management understand the socio-political reality of the relationship between social class and the political relations between capital and labor. The fact that people cannot be separated from human capital is crucial and requires its inseparability from principles.

From this perspective, information shapes the most important factors of production in the categories of land, labor, capital, and energy. Sixth, the Bank encourages the exchange of information and applications between countries by creating virtual networks in areas such as education, health, governance, the environment, agriculture and finance. This is necessary if countries are to become internationally competitive and realize the benefits that they and the region can derive from the information revolution.

This paper of Stal Paliwoda and Peterkosz highlights the role of the teaching methods in the development of human capital and the development of soft skills for students. The paper in the social dimension illustrates how the promotion of education can help people improve their soft skills, an important aspect of human and social capital.

Human capital is an intangible asset that is not listed on a company's balance sheet but includes things such as employee experience and skills. Because work is not considered equivalent, employers can improve human capital by investing in education and training that benefits their employees. For example, if Company X invests $2 million in its human capital and generates a total return of $1.5 million, managers can compare the return of their human capital year after year to track the return and improve their relationship with human capital investment.

Hardt and Negri (2000) argue that the term "human capital" is a new concept that transforms the whole human being into a type of capital. With telework and flexible working hours, workers can come under the influence of capital, and there is a possibility that people can be influenced by capital around the clock.

Human capital encompasses skills, education, talent, habits, and personal networks that enable individuals to generate income. No other country today has the resources that the United States has. To maximize this advantage and ensure that the US does not lose a step, it would be wise for politics and business to focus on America's human capital above all else.

# How Politics Influences Human Capital

Consumer spending and business investment not only boost economic growth, but also play a prominent role in determining workers' levels of education and development. The knowledge and skills of its people provide economic value, and skilled labor leads to higher productivity. The continuation of formal education from early childhood through the formal school system to adult education programmes and informal learning and work experience represents an investment in human capital.

I find a direct positive link between democratic and basic human capital, a negative link between regime stability and basic human capital, and between state instability and governance and a negative and positive link between advanced human capital. I also find an indirect positive effect of governance on democracy on both the types of human capital and its impact on income. Finally, I argue that there are significant indirect effects of democracy on growth, public health and education.

To test the sensitivity of our results to sampling I conclude that democracy is positively linked to basic human capital while regime instability negatively linked to it. Moreover, the results show that the effects of political and institutional variables vary between autocracies and democracies. Results also show that in a sample of developed countries, the democratic indicator covariance of the democracy indicator has a significant relation to human capital.

Econometric results suggest that the establishment of a democratic regime affects economic growth, but this effect affects variables that measure political institutions. The more democratic the regime, the longer political power is exercised by a particular political leader, and the more economic growth is handled, whereas in autocracies such effects are reversed. After examining other economic variables, Pereira and Tele (2010) found that political institutions play a role in emerging democracies, but not in consolidated democracies.

To assess the importance of political institutions for economic growth, Pereira and Tele (2010) developed an econometric model using a system of GMM estimates (autoregressive, distributed and delayed) that used annual data from a large sample of 109 countries for a maximum period of 1975-2004. That model bears out the same results using similar but unique data sets.

But most indicators of political institutions contain measurement errors. Most studies use enrollment rates or the average school years as indicators of human capital, assuming that human capital is a one-dimensional concept. Studies also use arbitrary policy indicators. This research uses two different measures of human capital, both of which aim to measure the impact of the quality and quantity of human capital in education on a country's economic growth.

For example, a change of government is possible in the coming years. So, understand the priorities of the new governments in terms of markets, industries and companies in order to orient your strategy of organizational transformation. When planning, you must take into account anticipated changes in market budgets and the availability of suitable candidates as a result of current and expected political influences [1]. Shifts in local public opinion, changes in government and the entry of the new superpowers of the industrial world into market policy can influence how much money is available, how much taxes are paid, minimum wage rates and market controls on the quality and quantity of available staff.

Many academics, practitioners and experts in human resources management agree that there is a phenomenon in which the political environment affects human capital resources in Kenya. Akongo and Dimba (2010) note that the political influence that the ruling party and the opposition have created in Kenya influences the process of raising human capital. This phenomenon is particularly pronounced in the structure of the public service, where many staff positions are influenced by various factors.

Due to the different political influences generated by the current political climate in Kenya, human capital procurement may suffer from negativity, tribalism, and other prejudices. Such phenomena that affect the business environment, such as belonging to particular communities or the perception of alignment with particular political parties, can also affect the dynamics of human capital.

The larger problem is the enormous importance of informal education, knowledge, and know-how beyond market activity, and the inability to individualize the shared pool of knowledge and skills that underlies productive innovation. For example, it is accepted that evaluation methods that focus on individual returns on education spending are limited because they focus too much on individual human capital, rather than aggregating it and measuring population. This heterogeneity is used by Uneces as a justification for rejecting cost-based approaches to assessing human capital that focus only on the sum of depreciating education spending, rather than discounting lifelong income - a method that reflects the true economic benefits of such spending.

With a focus on human capitalism, an organisation will recruit and compensate the most qualified staff possible, invest in their development, effectively manage them and, if possible, retain them for the long term. Human resources are promoted and achieved through mutual commitment and material investment, and the organisation favours and repays its members with a high level of performance.

Human Capitalism The concept of human capital derives from an economic model of human capital that emphasizes the relation between better productivity and performance and the need for continuous, long-term investment in human resource development. In this model, which is widely applied, investment in human capital is seen as having an impact on both national and global economic performance, and investment in people is also seen as crucial to an organization's performance. After investment, the initial Human Capital Coefficient remains positive and robust, confirming the new growth hypothesis that human capital is of considerable importance as an indicator of economic growth.

In the case of initial per capita income, the results are fragile and sensitive to the control variables contained in regression. They point to little importance in explaining per capita economic growth. Therefore human capital has other elements that cannot be defined by income alone.

## Is There A Perfect Human Capital Management System?

In my independent review of human capital management software I chose SuccessFactors as the best option for companies focusing on talent management because of its comprehensive functionality, strong track record and high investment in research and development. I also recommend SuccessFactor for its comprehensive Talent Management functionality, with additional emphasis on business execution, enterprise social and employee profile functionality.

HCM systems are the future of work, and life. If your workplace seems intrusive now, just wait until it includes one of the latest HCM systems. What does an HCM system look like exactly?

It has many features you would expect from a human resource management software such as applicant tracking, time tracking, timetables, onboarding, performance management system, HR workflows and much more. You can choose a solution that covers the strategic areas of human resources management, training, development and performance management as well as recruitment. Depending on your needs, you can opt for a simple HR software that has functions that take over the daily administrative tasks of employee management or leave the management to someone else.

This includes performance onboarding, analytics, position control, absence management and other human resources services. Workforce management software is ideal for planning, managing and tracking employees' work, including work requirements, employee schedules and paid leisure. An HCM platform has many advantageous automated functions such as recruitment, administration of administrative tasks such as salary and redundancy plans, and monitoring of employee performance and training.

Human capital management software is designed to manage and manage the workforce with ease and to increase employee experience and engagement. Human capital management includes traditional human resources practices such as payroll, reporting, employee tracking, performance management, personnel planning, training and development. Human resources management functions are involved in the recruitment, placement, evaluation, remuneration and development of employees in an organisation.

A Human Resources Management System (HRM) is software designed to manage payslips, monitor employees' travel, take time off and manage workloads. HR management software provides a platform on which different systems and processes can be combined to ensure that employees are accessible and that data is stored securely. Integrated human resources management software provides multiple modules to support the Human Resource Management organization, such as a payroll module, benefits management module, time and attendance module, talent management module and self-service learning management module.

Human resources management software ensures that all communication channels between employees and management are known and where employees can raise complaints and complaints. In addition, human capital management systems allow managers to create reports on their employees performance and provide templates for the use of the information accessed in the system.

Many companies use performance management systems to coach employees across their skill level and maturity, to organize and track performance evaluations and to receive weekly pulse updates. HR managers, managers and employees can focus with a performance management software platform on assessing skills, goals and performance of their employees and tracking improvements over time. This information gives HR managers, employees and managers a clear insight into the maturity and current role of an employee.

The processes companies use to recruit, support, and oversee employees cover all parts of their lifecycle: training, onboarding, wage and benefit management, and exit interviews. Remember that you should distinguish between the two: HR management does not include the different HR tasks and work practices, but the skills of HR management that improve the performance of the organization. Cloud-based enterprise-level HR software integrates, streamlines and automates human capital management processes such as recruitment, performance reviews, compensation management and employee development.

Instead of remitting to separate programs and processes, reliable HCM software offers a way to manage everything on one platform. It's accessible and quick for customer service teams, and it's highly customizable once you get the hang of it.

In the current age of digital transformation, companies must ensure that every important aspect of their business can benefit from various technological solutions to increase efficiency and foster the innovation at their disposal. Using technological solutions such as HRM can help you save time, reduce costs and better manage your employees.

Human Capital Management (HCM) is an approach to staffing that sees people as an asset and human capital as a fair value that can be measured for future value-adding investments. Often referred to as a business plan or policy area, it includes various IT applications and technical solutions to support the human resources department and enable them to implement their strategy. Because people and software are driven to make work easier, it is possible to develop a Human Capital Management System (HCMS) to alleviate management fatigue, reduce employee frustration and improve company performance.

Human Resource Information Systems (HRIS) is a software generic term that covers many different types of software and software companies. These products are known for the storage of individual employee data, managing salary and benefit management and managing regulatory, legal, and labor requirements of a company under many different names. Today, HCM platforms are not just transaction and employee experience systems; they are also real-time analytics systems, predictive performance tools and employee voice systems that help employees speak out when work needs to change.

Taken together, this means that the introduction of such a uniform system will have a profound impact on the functioning of human resources departments. Many providers have convinced their customers that their systems will make their companies more agile. Integrating data will improve decision-making, but many promised improvements fall on the shoulders of your management and not on the "systems" of software vendors.

Instead of completing one task after another with a combination of paper documentation and multiple digital systems, each has its own issues and login requirements. A human capital management platform enables all this within a single ecosystem, enabling human resources managers to concentrate on helping new employees handle the forms themselves rather than on the system requirements they can access.

As authorities respond and respond to these changes, the post-pandemic workplace offers new opportunities to fill the technological, skills, and experience gaps that have made hiring and retaining government workers a challenge for decades.

The HCM software not only gives staff the tools to better manage talent, but also enables employees to realise their full potential, fosters stronger links with managers and creates a work culture that makes sense and coordinates projects and skills. It also contributes to improving efficiency through self-service automation, enabling staff to better understand and collaborate with employees on "well-being and commitment, prepare for the future and align people and resources with the mission of today's organization. Government and IT leaders can use HCM technology to drive broader organizational change.

# How Has Covid-19 Changed Human Capital?

The performance of remote workers depends on managers understanding what is required to manage remote teams (Aitken, Fox and others, cited in 2020b Aitken & Fox, Coffey, Dayaram, Fitzgerald, Gupta, McKenna, Wei & Tian, 2020b ). The success of remote work depends on the understanding and virtual monitoring of employees by managers (Aitken, Fox, et al, referenced in an it isken, fox, coffey, dayaram, fitzgerald, gupta, mckenna, wei, & tian, 2020a, b). The impact on employee health varies depending on the working environment and occupational role of employees (Brooks & Dunn, Amlot, Rubin & Greenberg, Referees in Brooks & Dunn, Amlot, Rubins & Greenberg, 2018).

CEOs should see workers as an important stakeholder crucial to recovery in view of COVID-19 and its impact on human health and economy. This brings human capital governance to the fore, and boards of directors should invite investors and regulators to monitor human capital issues. Investors can assess an organization's effectiveness in limiting Covid 19 human capital risks and those with an established human capital and governance framework can be confident that they are well positioned to create long-term value.

Regulators such as the Securities and Exchange Commission are urging companies to disclose the measures they take to protect their human capital in the upcoming earnings reports. Companies with well-established human capital governance frameworks are considered better investors and more prepared to create long-term value, and regulators such as the US Securities and Exchange Commission are urging them to disclose the measures they have taken to protect employees' " health in coming earnings releases. Another change that has occurred during the COVID 19 crisis is that employees increasingly see the Board of Directors as a key stakeholder in the economic recovery.

The pandemic has restructured the way organizations manage their human capital. The COVID-19 pandemic changed the way they segmented their workforce, including the indispensable front-line workers. It accelerated the pace at which organizations were changing their compensation programs, salary reductions, incentive resets, and bonuses.

The COVID 19 pandemic has forced HR managers to rethink the way they communicate with staff. In this blog you will learn how Covid-19 changed the way companies communicate and support their employees. Download our eBook, 10 Principles of Modern Employee Communication to learn how to communicate with modern employees in today's digital age.

Organizations that provide clear, concise, and continuous communication help employees feel prepared instead of panicking. Other employers have been slow to respond and haven't given sufficient specific guidance to reassure employees, said Carla Bevin, a professor of corporate communications at the Tepper School of Business at Carnegie Mellon University.

Recognizing the gap between words and acts, a group of institutional investors formed the Human Capital Management Coalition (HCMC), which has been advocating for improved HCM disclosure by the SEC since 2017. Building on HCMC's work, a broader investor coalition led by the Interfaith Center for Corporate Responsibility in April signed a statement calling on companies to respond to COVID-19 by focusing on the well-being of their employees.

In the age of social distancing and increasing distance work, for example, companies are realigning their talent strategies and redeploying their workforce. In the future, organizations are likely to look for meaningful ways to measure culture and to show progress. From remote work and health services to employee morale and disaster planning, HR experts are determined to help their organizations move forward.

Consider how much changed we have had in the eight months since COVID-19 was declared a pandemic by the World Health Organization (WHO). The future of work is already underway, and the Covid-19 pandemic has accelerated it.

The responses to the coronavirus are instructive for companies and sectors seeking change in the Fourth Industrial Revolution. Investors should assess the lessons learned from the pandemic and incorporate them into their active ownership efforts in sectors that seek to manage the immediate future business opportunities and human capital risks and impacts in the context of COVID-19.

Recent events have reminded individuals and companies that they depend on human beings for essential functions, illustrating the fragile state of many professions. COVID-19 has highlighted the role and impact on workers. This extraordinary pandemic highlighted the importance of pro-active business planning and robust risk management systems as companies are tested on their ability to respond to shocks and adapt to changing circumstances.

In fact, organizations are not always ready to deal with a crisis when it occurs, as Wang, Hutchins, and Garavan mention in their article. Many measures and decisions are arbitrary, but Strategic Human Resources Management (HRM) needs to be taken and enforced, such as ensuring employee health and safety, implementing new work agreements, maintaining employee morale and commitment, and dealing with cuts and layoffs. Knowledge of how HRP handles crises, especially in the early stages of the COVID 19 pandemic, is useful in identifying specific measures that HRP can be helpful but not resilient in a crisis like this.

Crises are nothing new for organizations, but COVID-19 has presented vigilant, responsive, adaptable and crisis-ready organizations with unexpected challenges of unprecedented magnitude. The pandemic has changed the lifestyles of most people and forced countries, societies, businesses and individuals to rethink how they live and work.

In the age of human capital, workers have become assets that must be nurtured at the expense of administration. The Shareholder Value Age is a zero-sum game in which many are driven to zero. With the efficiencies achieved by using technology to replace human labor with technology platforms, reduce personnel costs, and shift work to contract and gig workers, we are running out of shareholder value before the era ends.

The temporary nature of flexible employment also poses a challenge for employee retention. In the age of shareholder value, it is a nice idea for companies to put employees at the door and retrain them for new and necessary activities.

In order to support an online work environment, employers start digitizing their human capital management and implement various solutions for the collaboration, communication, productivity, feedback and talent generation of employees, among other things. Most employers are also updating their crisis management strategies to prepare for crises such as the current pandemic.

## How Will Human Capital Change In The Future?

Brainstorming initiatives HR managers should look for ways to close the gaps in employee experience through technology. For example, if data from the exit survey shows that employees leave your company due to lack of development opportunities, you should invest in Learning Management Systems (LMS) to create development paths for your workforce. The information collected by assessing employee needs, such as employee retention software, surveys, exit interviews and employee suggestions boxes, can be used to recommend initiatives to improve employee experience.

Human resources and business partners who can articulate human resources needs to management should consider themselves as internal service providers to ensure a high return on human capital investment. To facilitate this shift to talent management, we need to build analytical capacities that mine data to recruit, develop, and retain the best people. For example, executives can be involved in regular talent reviews, and HR managers and business partners can develop semi-automatic data dashboards to track key metrics for key roles.

Technology cannot replace human creativity, collaboration, and problem-solving skills. The second step for HR managers is to find places where people can thrive in their organizations. These are areas where people in your organization can add real value and it makes sense to recruit and develop people who are strong in these areas because your workforce already does more than technology can't.

On a practical level, human resources experts will not be able to carry out effective human resources planning to recruit, hire and train the right talent, say experts. Human resources experts need to understand the business operations of the company. In addition to knowing the share price of the company and reading the profit and loss account, personnel must also understand the strategic direction of the company and the economic and social environment in which it operates.

Corporate governance can help improve the health and well-being of its employees while maintaining transparency and clear communication within their organization. Reid advises small business owners to set a good example by taking time for themselves and setting limits and expectations for your team to follow suit. The search for new leadership affects the entire company, and HR executives can play a key role in steering their companies in the right direction.

New technologies present new challenges for employees and personnel managers. In the age of social distancing and increasing distance work, for example, companies are realigning their talent strategies and redeploying their workforce. HR managers must aim to maintain the corporate culture of the company, improve employee motivation and engagement, keep pace with the demands of new millennials, and provide better learning opportunities for employees.

Investing in and prioritising human capital in these six areas will help organisations mitigate the risks and negative impacts of COVID-19. Boards should take a long-term view of the future of work and ensure that their organisations cope with the changing workplace environment. Companies that accelerate future work and promote human capital with efficient, agile and targeted resources will reduce risks and increase competitiveness and profitability.

To answer these questions, Deloitte has released an influential report that reflects how companies will respond to the enormous challenges of the technological revolution. To this end, they consulted with industry leaders and experts to learn the most important HR trends for 2021 so that managers can make informed decisions for their businesses. Faced with changing priorities, companies are changing their way of working and the actual organisation of the company.

McKinsey recently conducted an investigation into how companies will organize themselves in the future. According to this influential report, companies have been rated as responding to the enormous challenges of the technological revolution and 88% of respondents (10,000 entrepreneurs and human resources managers from 140 countries) rated building the organization of the future as the most important. In an article of the International Monetary Fund (more on this later), author Branco Milanovic noted that the main reason for the shift in the decade 2011 was the concern that income inequality is dampening economic growth and the increasing importance of human capital development.

A country value of 0.70 on the human capital index is a value that indicates the future earning potential of a child born today: 70% if he or she has completed an education and is in full health. Accessible education is difficult to achieve in an income-distributed society. It is important that there is a large contingent of rich people who save a larger share of their income than the poor and invest in physical capital.

The Human Capital Index (HCI) measures the contribution of health, education and productivity to the next generation of workers. A country value of 0.50 for future GDP per worker is the highest for a country that has achieved the benchmark of complete education and health. The index links these scenarios to the future incomes of countries and individuals.

The Human Capital Index 2020 (HCI) covers 174 countries, 17 more than when it was launched in 2018. Not surprising though, HCI levels vary widely for MENA countries, from 0.67 in the United Arab Emirates (UAE) to 0.37 in Yemen. In conflict-affected countries such as Iraq and Yemen, the low index raises important questions about how to support human capital protection and improve in the midst of conflict.

Strong efforts are needed to preserve the human capital of displaced persons and refugees and to promote social inclusion and economic mobility. Second, many MENA countries have shown a keen focus on protecting human capital since the pandemic outbreak by increasing the transfers and strengthening social safety nets.

It is important that all industries try to find their way around and create optimal working conditions and premises. It must take into account a company's contribution to society, both as a customer and as an employee. The participation complements the World Bank Group's long-standing engagement with countries and sectors that contribute to human development.

# In Which Areas Of The Economy Will Human Capital Always Be Necessary?

Productivity growth slowed from 2.5% per year between 1995 and 2010 to 0.4% between 2011 and 2015, which worries economists, because productivity is a key factor in economic growth, real wages, and living standards. Researchers estimate that educational attainment has increased by about a year per decade, contributing about 0.6 percentage points to annual productivity growth.7 They warn that if that growth slows, it could mean that the growing contribution to economic growth, and thus to income, will decline.

Human capital theory is based on the assumption that formal education is instrumental and necessary to improve a population's productivity. In short, human capital theorists argue that a well-educated population is a more productive population. Studies that find that education correlates with economic growth argue that the causality of education goes from education to growth, which is consistent with the growth model of human capital.

Human capital theory emphasizes that education increases workers' productivity and efficiency by increasing the cognitive stock - that is the productive human capacity - that is the product of innate skills and investment in people. Governments have long recognized that the knowledge that people gain from education can help develop economies and boost economic growth. Modern economists seem to agree that education and health care are key to improving human capital and boosting a nation's economic performance (Becker 1993).

The knowledge and skills of its people provide economic value, and skilled labor leads to higher productivity. Workers with higher education and skills tend to have higher incomes, which in turn boosts economic growth through increased consumer spending. Labour productivity growth is influenced by savings, investment in physical capital, the expansion of human capital and the discovery of new technologies.

An economy that includes new ideas and technologies that improve the standard of living requires that the workers implement and manage these new technologies. An economy is considered healthy if it has high employment, stable prices and sustainable growth. Individuals, businesses and organisations do better when they contribute to the success of the economy as a whole.

Nobel Prize-winning economist Gary Becker explained the relation between human capital and economic growth when he wrote: "Economic growth depends on the synergy between new knowledge and human capital and when significant gains in education and training are accompanied by significant advances in technological knowledge, countries can achieve considerable economic growth". Research has shown that investing in human capital through formal and informal vocational training and development programs leads to higher business performance, higher productivity, employee loyalty and innovation. With these objectives in mind, the World Bank launched the Human Capital Project, a program of advocacy, measurement and analysis to raise awareness and increase demand for interventions to build human capital.

The lack of physical capital in countries with surplus labour can be solved by accelerating the formation of human capital through private and public investments in the education and health sectors of their economies. Human resources can be transformed into human capital through effective inputs such as education, health, and moral values. The transformation of human resources into productive human resources through these inputs is the process of human capital formation.

Recent US research has shown that geographical regions that invest in human capital and the economic progress of immigrants living in their countries are helping to boost their short- and long-term economic growth. Based on the results of previous research, we recommend that an analysed company focus on the relationship between labor productivity and reward systems, focusing on the needs of the specific human capital as it is able to create value through human capital. It is also important that the analysed company pays attention to Human Capital Value Added (HCVA) as it indicates the total efficiency and utilisation of human resources and value creation work. We conclude from these results that the company is effectively using its human resources.

The Human Capital Index measures the productivity of the next generation of workers relative to a measure of completed education and total health. Companies with a higher proportion of skilled workers can innovate faster than individuals without strong human capital and generate higher economic returns from new technologies. When variables related to social skills are incorporated into econometric models of human capital, the growth level of human capital becomes significant.

This provides an implicit empirical specification of the need to include other channels through which human capital influences economic growth. Based on the endogenous growth literature, this underlines the importance of integrating different channels beyond social skills and human capital, which also influence economic growth.

The task is to measure the intermediate factors that influence these results. The most prominent suspects are socioeconomic and institutional indicators, factors that can influence the quality of human capital accumulation and strengthen or weaken the relationship between human capital and growth.

The main assumption of educational research is the idea that the education system is the main driver of change in society as a whole. For example, secondary education is presented as an agency for economic development, and most official documents recognize the existence of a correlation between the rising number of secondary school graduates and economic progress (Watson 1967).

Not surprisingly, research and politics developed currents that saw education as an important institution shaping general development. This common paradigm of educational research and policy was accompanied by the study of the universalization of compulsory education and the struggle to transform the upper-secondary elite into the mass on the general level.

## In Which Areas Of The Economy Will Human Capital Be Reduced?

Eventually, many parts of the economy will be automated. Jobs will become redundant and less educated people will be less numerous in the workforce.This is because educated and educated people are able to be more productive in the workplace. The quality of qualifications is difficult to measure in terms of production performance. But workers are trained to be productive for the sake of their moral and spiritual well-being.

A well-educated, innovative and creative workforce contributes to increasing labour productivity and economic growth. In the age of globalization there was a large movement of workers that allowed skilled workers to move to high-income countries from low-income countries. Not only does the US economy have a better educated workforce and better physical capital than it did a few decades ago, but it also has access to more advanced technology.

Since the late 1950's, economists have conducted growth accounting studies to determine how deepening physical and human capital, as well as technology, contribute to growth. The usual approach is to use the aggregate productive function to estimate how much economic growth can be attributed to the growth of physical capital relative to human capital.

While investment in physical capital is essential for growth of labor productivity and per capita GDP, building up human capital is at least as important. The growth of human and physical capital accounts for less than half of the economic growth that is taking place. Human capital influences economic growth by contributing to the development of the economy by increasing people's knowledge and skills.

Human capital refers to the knowledge, skills and experience of workers in an economy. The knowledge and skills of its people provide economic value, and skilled labor leads to higher productivity. Human capital provides employers with entrepreneurial impetus through training and other forms of investment, which are of economic value not only for the company but also the country's economy as a whole.

Increasing labour productivity has been recognised as a key factor in boosting economic growth and reducing poverty in Latin America. Increasing productivity tends to increase profitability, which means that investing in employees produces positive results when it matters most. The human capital component has been shown to have a positive impact on poverty alleviation.

At the same time, a well-educated population is able to address other problems that arise in society. The continuation of formal education from early childhood through the formal school system to adult education programmes and informal learning and work experience represents an investment in human capital. The training of workers is seen as very important and many private companies offer training programmes.

Governments recognize that the knowledge that people gain through education helps developing countries and boosts economic growth. Workers with higher education and skills tend to have higher incomes, which in turn boosts economic growth by additional consumer spending.

Changes in skill and wage structures in the labour market are an important part of the evidence. Human capital has deepened overall among US workers, and shows that the share of the US population with a high school or college degree has increased.

A recent article examining the relation between human capital and economic growth found that human capital explains between 10% and 30% of the difference in the per capita income between countries. The positive effects of human capital gains have continued over time, underscoring their importance to the state and society, improving people's quality of life as an intrinsic value, increasing sustainability, productivity, and, for economic growth, as an instrumental value. The company increases the capital level per person, which leads to a so-called capital deepening.

Adam Smith defined four types of investment capital, which are characterised by the fact that they allow income and profits to circulate without switching between the gents.

When economies try to break out of a stable state, they tend to return to low levels, and this is called a poverty trap. There are countries in poverty traps in Sub-Saharan Africa, where human capital is low and the incidence of infectious diseases is high. Even with an influx of foreign human capital, it may not be enough to break the critical value of HM, and even if it returns to HM in the long term, it still will be in a so-called 'poverty trap'.

The EU 2020 strategy focuses on smart, sustainable and inclusive growth that is impossible to achieve without the important contribution of skills, knowledge and human values, the so-called human capital. The problem of shortages of physical capital and surplus labor in countries can be solved by accelerating the formation of human capital through private and public investments in education and health sectors as well as by surpluses in their economies. The transformation of human resources into productive human resources is most effective when inputs such as education, health and moral values are in the process of forming human capital.

In companies, they are called talent management or human resources. The added value of raw materials and manufacturing processes is based on a highly skilled and innovative workforce.

Countries with a high informal rate (34% in Turkey and 60% in Peru) suggest that the formal sector cannot absorb a large percentage of the workforce for several reasons, including low human capital. Although the participation of people with higher education in the labor force is higher than in previous generations, countries like Peru face challenges in the quality of their human capital, limiting productivity growth.

## In Which Areas Of The Economy Will Human Capital Be Eliminated?

Human capital influences economic growth by helping an emerging economy expand its people's knowledge and skills. Cuaresma, Doppelhofer and Feldkircher (2012) found taking into account a wide range of geographical, institutional and cultural variables of human capital that human capital is the most important factor for regional development. In two of its key outcomes, capital grew faster in some regions than in others, and human capital in higher education was the most robust driver of economic growth.

The knowledge and skills of its people provide economic value, and skilled labor leads to higher productivity. Human resources can be transformed into human capital through effective inputs such as education, health, and moral values. Human capital refers to the knowledge, skills and experience of workers in an economy.

The transformation of human resources into productive human resources with effective use of education, health and moral values is a process of human capital formation. In the long term, employers and employees must invest in the development of human capital, not only for the organisations and their clientele, but also for the benefit of society as a whole. The shortage of physical capital and labour surpluses in some countries can be solved by accelerating human capital production through private and public investments in the education and health sectors as well as surpluses in their economies.

Investors, lenders, suppliers and other market participants who want to evaluate a company want detailed, reliable, consistent and comparable information about its employees, from the C-suite to the factory floor. A strong workforce is a source of competitive advantage, and effective labor management and investment in human capital are quantifiable organizational assets that will create future profits and contribute to overall growth. For employers, investments in human capital include commitments to training workers, training programs, training bonuses and benefits, family assistance funds, and higher education scholarships.

To understand the value and prospects of a company, one must understand how it uses its resources. Consumer spending and business investment not only enhance economic growth, but also play a prominent role in determining workers' levels of education and development. Knowledge, education, experience, health, diversity and other characteristics that influence the productivity of a company's employees have a significant impact on its value, profitability and prospects, including its ability to innovate and to remain resilient over the long term.

In the course of training the workforce, another type of investment is capital investment, such as investment in equipment in human capital. Human capital is strongly correlated with economic growth, and investment tends to increase productivity. There are many theories linking investments in human capital with the development of education and the role of human capital in economic development, productivity growth and innovation are often cited as justification for government grants to education and vocational training.

The role of the state is key to raising the skill and education levels of a rural population. For example, some countries offer their citizens free higher education, recognizing that an educated population tends to earn more, spend more, and boost the economy. A recent study found that the best educated in the Arab world are best prepared to work in the global economy.

Policymakers should therefore pay close attention to the development of human capital in order to adapt the skills of the population to the needs of the labour market and the quality of education. Deficits in these areas threaten to undermine progress in creating the type of society - a knowledge and information society - that is necessary to address the complex problems of the 21st century relating to the well-being and development of the community. A study funded by RAND Corporation documents measures that four countries - Lebanon, Oman, Qatar and the United

Arab Emirates (UAE) - have taken to address human capital learning skills, skills and knowledge problems as well as individual labor market issues.

It should be noted that the direct role of human capital, although limited, has a major indirect impact on growth due to its impact on technological progress and the implementation of growth-promoting institutions (Glaeser, La Porta, Lopez-Silane & Shleifer, 2004 ). The growth model of the poverty trap is consistent with the reality that developing countries can allow the level of human capital to exceed the critical value (HM) of the trap to escape. An influx of foreign human capital is described as a poverty trap, even if it is not enough to break the deadlock if it brings the world back in the long run.

The idea of deepening human capital also applies to workers' years of experience, and the average level of experience of US workers has barely changed in recent decades. For example, in 1970, half of American adults had at least a high school diploma, by the beginning of the 20th century more than 80% of adults had finished high school. The U.S. Patent and Trademark Office has granted more than 150,000 patents in recent years.

# How Are Robotics Changing Human Capital?

When people hear the term "artificial intelligence" their first thought is robotics doing their jobs, but that is not the case. True, automation, robotics, and other cutting-edge solutions assume the need for human intervention and implementation, but they divert, not replace, human jobs. Robotics and machine learning, along with their related technological cousins, chatbots and AI, have left many people fearful that they will one day lose their jobs.

We are witnessing a robotic takeover of a multitude of tasks and jobs from self-driving cars to medical diagnoses. In the workplace, robotics and machine learning already confuse everything from billing to customer service, and new research from Pegasystem suggests that employees expect to work more and more in these areas.

With so many experts predicting robotic revolution and automation trends, one would think that it is time for organizations to prepare for the invasion of robots and artificial intelligence. For many, the prospect of being replaced by robots or artificial intelligence programs is a fear on the horizon.

In a scenario in which 60% of jobs are lost to automation and robots, the human resources management sector may have to adapt to massive job losses and the need to retrain and retrain the workforce. Automation and robotics will lead to a change in the way human resources work, a reduction in the size of the workforce and the possibility of redundancies as routine processes are automated and robots replace staff. It's no longer an "if" that robots start taking over jobs, it's a quota that human resources managers need to change.

This does not mean that rules-based, repetitive jobs will be at the lower end of the scale: technology is evolving rapidly to take on complex jobs in the economy because it follows a well-defined logic with a high level of consistency and predictability. This leaves a whole host of other jobs open to human labor, jobs that require skills like empathy and problem solving that only humans today have and will continue to monopolize in the foreseeable future. The technological shift to automation and artificial intelligence requires new educational initiatives to create a mix of people with the right technology, emotional and social skills that require fewer physical and manual skills.

Fred Goff, CEO of Jobcase, notes that as automation and robotics increase, working in office environments means expanding access to educational opportunities, giving workers a way to reshape themselves and their careers.

The growth of automation and robotics is creating new employment opportunities in many industrial sectors. Training to ensure employees are programmed to install, operate and maintain machines will continue to grow as demand grows for more automation. Automation and its penetration and complexity will also increase.

For example, software robots penetrate the business world by using robotics and process automation (RPA) to block repetitive and predictable jobs. RPA handles mundane and boring tasks, such as data entry and spreadsheet creation, that can be performed by robots, not humans.

For example, many companies already have automated systems for advising their employees on financial planning, available to large employers and used by asset management companies with hundreds of advisers. As already mentioned, many people who will be replaced by robots will have to monitor the work of the robots in order to ensure optimum efficiency. As a rule, a range of repetitive, repetitive types of work can be automated, whether they are human resources offices, factory halls or self-driving vehicles.

Software bots and sophisticated algorithms also make it easier for recruiters to find and screen applicants - functions traditionally performed by human resources workers. Nearly half of business leaders surveyed said automation will lead to fewer employees in 2020, compared with a quarter who said so in 2017.

Automation creeps in and involves the use of machines to replace inefficient, repetitive, or risky aspects of a job, or technology to improve functions that remain in human hands.

Recent economic research suggests that technology is only one aspect of the gain in value. 67 percent of CEOs said they believe that technology will provide more value for human capital in a Korn Ferry Global survey of 800 top executives. Among the results of the survey, 44 percent of respondents said that the growth of robotics, automation and artificial intelligence will make people irrelevant in the future.

An economic analysis commissioned by Korn Ferry has shown that human capital will have greater value for organizations in the future. Human capital represents a potential value of $1.2 trillion, or 233 times physical capital.

As human resources professionals look towards the future, their primary goal should be to rethink what we need to do as a workforce to adopt the latest HR technologies, reinvent the role of human resources and highlight the importance of a future-ready workforce to drive these changes. As found in the 2018 Deloitte's Human Capital Trends Report 2018, the adoption of automation, robotics and artificial intelligence in the workplace is accelerating, providing a real opportunity to rethink our work models in ways that maximize the value of humans and machines. I think that the next wave of innovation will help us retain our own relevance and add value to the foreseeable robotized economy by harnessing AI's ability to increase our contributions, maximize our potential and put us on the right track.

In this age, human-assisted AI, equipped with judgment and empathy skills to optimize human capital, can measure our learning curve and readiness to enable a continuous symbiosis between individual self-realization and structural changes in industries that are accompanied by emerging needs and skills. The future is murky and it will take effort and evangelization, but human resources can play a crucial role for businesses as this type of technology can help people learn how to work with automation, for example, and help us make meaningful use of human-machine collaboration.

# How Is Artificial Intelligence Replacing Human Capital?

As artificial intelligence and robots join more work teams, humans will have to adapt, acquire new skills, and take on new roles. Nurses, for example, will use smart systems to manage paperwork and do more with their time, freeing up patients for care. This difference in skills means that, over the next decade, human resource managers must focus on shaping the workforce to increase human numbers, not replace them with artificial intelligence.

HRs main focus is on the deconstruction of workplaces to determine which tasks can be automated or expanded by AI and which gaps humans need to fill. AI-driven jobs require employees to nurture the talents that humans already possess. Tasks such as recruiting and onboarding new types of employees will be affected by AI but will not be replaced without people interviewing and meeting potential employees to determine things such as culture, fit, and personality.

AI and robots are not a substitute for manpower; rather, roles are being abolished and new ones created.

Artificial intelligence will never replace the human element needed to make decisions that robots and machines can never make. With technology and the resulting data, dealing with it will continue to be a challenge for HR managers, departments and other employees as companies increasingly have more data and automation available for a variety of roles. Collecting employee data, such as during the RiseSmart layoffs, can give the company's HR managers a better understanding of things like alumni sentiment, changes in notification practices, and providing resilience training to remaining employees, but human touch will never fully replace the machine.

On the positive side for HR professionals, the disruption of HR tasks and processes caused by AI can reinforce HR tasks and processes rather than replace them by recommending that HRM should be completed by humans. Most experts say that robotic process automation (RPA) can lead to efficiency gains by negating the need for manual processes and data entry. Even the most difficult tasks, considered boring and repetitive in the hands of AI systems, can be handled in a way that affects practitioners' time and reduces problems caused by human error.

In a report, Gartner noted that AI is expected to create 2.3 million additional jobs, but will eliminate more than 1.8 million jobs, especially in middle and lower management positions. AI provides HR departments with the ability to improve applicant and employee experience through automating repetitive and cost-effective tasks - saving time to focus on the strategic and creative work that HR teams need and want to do. For companies where people are critical to success, SAGE HR can help companies overcome the complexity of managing their employees so they can concentrate on growing their business.

Instead of monitoring every step of the new employee onboarding process, these tasks can be automated, adds Bokel-Herd, allowing teams to devote more time to more important tasks such as mentoring and feedback.

According to Emily He, the SVP of Human Capital Management in the Oracle Cloud Business Group, the latest advances in machine learning and artificial intelligence are thriving in the mainstream. These developments are leading to a "massive, massive change in the way people around the world interact with technology and their teams," said he in a press release from Oracle's Future of Workplace Study. In labour force analysis and planning, AI and machine learning are becoming increasingly evident.

Robotics and machine learning, along with their related technological cousins, chatbots and AI, have raised fears among many people that they will one day lose their jobs. True, automation, robotics, and other cutting-edge solutions remove the need for human intervention, but they divert, not replace, human jobs. In the workplace, these technologies are already disrupting everything from customer accounts to customer care, and new research from

Pegasystem suggests that employees should be prepared to work alongside them.

According to the study, artificial intelligence plays a role in 55 percent of all human resources departments in international companies. Many fear that the rise of artificial intelligence will see machines and robots replacing human labor, but some see the advancement of technology as a threat rather than a tool to improve ourselves. According to Rosemary Haefner, Head of Human Resources at CareerBuilder, robots and AI will not replace the human element in human resources, but will shape the corporate culture.

While AI will remain a prominent buzzword now and in the future, companies need to recognize that self-learning black box skills are not a panacea. Many organizations are beginning to recognize and use artificial intelligence's incredible capabilities to enhance human intelligence and draw real value from their data. As we develop innovative technologies, artificial intelligence will have a positive impact on our economy, create jobs and bring the skills needed to introduce new systems.

In this age, human-assisted AI, endowed with judgment and empathy skills and human capital optimization, can measure our learning curve and readiness to enable a continuous symbiosis of individual self-realization and structural change in industries that are associated with emerging needs and capabilities. The future is a blur, and it will require effort and evangelization, but human resources will play a crucial role in companies of all kinds, because technology for example helps people learn to work with automation and helps us make good use of human-machine cooperation. What I believe should not be lost is that the next wave of innovation will help us maintain our own relevance and add value to the future robot-like economy by harnessing AI's ability to increase our contributions, to maximize our potential and to put us on the right track.

Artificial intelligence will change our world and the workplace. It will be able to analyse candidates with an open mind compared to the potential bias and fallibility of human resource responsibility.

The current evolution of AI and automation is changing the way we live and work, and the way we invest in human capital.

## Is It Possible For Robotics To Replace Human Capital?

According to leading experts from BMW Group and Deloitte, human workers will remain crucial in factories for the foreseeable future but will not be replaced by robots or artificial intelligence (AI). The Deloitte's Annual Human Capital Trends Study examines the ongoing dynamics between machine and man and the need for a combination of both to enable the workforce of the future. Advances in automation continue to gain momentum and accelerate in the face of the pandemic, but technology can also be used to enhance human efforts and complement them, resulting in safer and less repetitive roles for workers.

Robots have already replaced humans in many professions, and innovative agricultural equipment replaced human horses during the Industrial Revolution. The crisis caused by the pandemic should accelerate the transition to automation of certain production tasks, such as repetitive work, material handling, taxation and dangerous activities, as well as support and identification of quality deficiencies. The human being is expanded by robots in a way that leads to gains in productivity, efficiency and safety.

In the context of this book, and in the broader global context, "machine" describes a computer, computer-controlled equipment, or robot programmed to learn like a human. Sometimes we call it artificial intelligence (AI), sometimes we call it machine learning, and sometimes it's called robotic bot.

Robotics and machine learning, along with their related technological cousins, chatbots and AI, have raised fears among many people that they will one day lose their jobs. True, automation, robotics, and other cutting-edge solutions eliminate the need for human intervention, but the implementation of these technologies diverts, not replaces, human jobs. In the workplace, these technologies are already disrupting everything from customer accounts to customer care, and new research from Pegasystem suggests that employees should be prepared to work with them.

There is never a guarantee that technology will evolve without change, but human resources are in the best position to retain human labor. Automation is already replacing many jobs in many different industries, and people who want to enter human resources, or are currently employed in human resources, fear that automation will replace their jobs.

If you have a choice between robots and human employees, most companies choose robots because they are cheaper and more efficient. Robotics can benefit people in other industries and other areas of the country, including by lowering the cost of goods.

National economic benefits are another reason why researchers have calculated that adding a robot could replace 33% of all jobs in the country. The manufacturing jobs they replace come from segments of the workforce where there are many other goods and employment opportunities, leading to a direct link between the automation of robots used in these industries and workers' declining incomes.

This is consistent with the argument that robots are cheaper than human capital and can work 24 hours a day owing to significant overhead costs like overtime, health insurance and other benefits. Claims that machines destroy human labor are exaggerated, but research by Acemoglu and Restrepo shows that robotic effects, especially real ones in manufacturing, can have significant social repercussions. Although robotics is central to security details, there are a few reasons why human factors will never be fully replaced.

Automation and artificial intelligence (AI) are changing the world we live in and there are many concerns that robots are coming to our jobs. For example, a 2013 study by researchers at Oxford University estimated that up to half of all US jobs are at risk of automation over the next 20 years. The Wires's James Surowiecki points out that many employers see skill shortages, labor shortages and labor surpluses, and expect robots to take over jobs.

The Organization for Economic Cooperation and Development has stated that automation threatens

9% of all jobs in more than 21 countries. A recent headline I read suggested that machines could replace half of all human jobs. Scary stuff.

We can imagine Star Wars-style robots in the vein of R2-D2 and C-3PO, robot devices and algorithms that combine human and mechanical functions such as thermostats, dishwashers and search engines for air traffic. Besides physical capital in the form of technology, robots can be programmed to perform many tasks that do not require a human operator. Some workplaces, many of them, are vulnerable to automation, which means that technology is available to program production processes that would otherwise have to take place with human help. As computer processing becomes cheaper, it will be cost-effective for robots to do more routine tasks that could be done by humans.

An assembly line consists of a series of stations where five or six workers are responsible for mounting and attaching a particular part of the car frame so that it can move to the next station which has a further set of robot trailers instead of a human.

Given advancements in artificial intelligence (AI) and automation, the weight of this type of technology predicts that the potential is high for significant displacement of workers and further erosion of labor. These changes will replace and continue to replace jobs on which many workers, families and communities depend. However, the development of technologies that facilitate new tasks for which people are better suited could lead to a better future for workers.

What I believe will not be lost is that the next wave of innovation will help us to maintain our own relevance and add value to the foreseeable robotized economy by harnessing AI's ability to increase our contributions, maximize our potential and put us on the right track. In this age, we will use human-assisted AI, endowed with judgment and empathy skills, optimization of human capital to measure our learning curve and readiness to enable continuous symbiosis and individual self-realization, as well as structural changes in industries associated with emerging needs and skills.

The future is murky and requires effort and evangelization, but human resources will play a key role in companies of all kinds: technologies that teach people how to work with automation, or that help us understand and use the collaboration between man and machine.

# Is It Possible For Artificial Intelligence To Replace Human Capital?

The difference in skills between humans and AI means that, over the next decade, human resource managers must focus on designing the workforce to replicate, not replace, human beings with artificial intelligence. HRs will focus on cutting jobs, identifying what tasks can be automated or expanded by AI, and what gaps humans need to fill. AI-driven jobs require employees to nurture the talents that humans already possess.

Whether they are security staff, accountants, taxi drivers, lawyers, cashiers, stockbrokers, court reporters or pathologists - human workers in business will find that their skills will be in demand, their roles will be outdated, and sophisticated AI systems will perform these tasks cheaper than humans. AI and robots are not just about replacing workers, they are also about eliminating roles and creating new ones.

To mitigate the impact of job relocations, society will need to be nimble and resourceful in its policy responses. Meaningful investment in retraining and retraining by both public and private employers will be important to postpone the obsolescence of the human, worker-driven economy. In a world where materials goods and services are more readily available thanks to automation and where demand for remunerated human labor is scarce, a paradigm shift in how society imagines resource allocation will be necessary.

In her recently published article "AI and human intelligence in the future of work" I read that HR should think about the impact of AI automation of work tasks on key roles and work processes. The key to developing an AI automation strategy for HR managers is to start analyzing roles, processes, and workflows to retrain AI.

According to Emily He, SVP of Human Capital Management in Oracle's Cloud Business Group, the latest advances in machine learning and artificial intelligence reach mainstream applications. These developments "are leading to a massive, massive change in the way people around the world interact with technology and their teams," he said in a press release from the Future of Workplace Study by Oracle. In labour force analysis and planning, AI and machine learning are becoming increasingly evident.

Rapid advances in artificial intelligence (AI) and automation technologies have the potential to disrupt the labour market. The rise of automation comes at a time of growing economic inequality, fueling fears of mass technological unemployment and renewing calls for political efforts to address the effects of technological change. While AI and automation can increase some workers' productivity, they can also replace the work done by others and transform occupations, at least to some extent.

Robotics and machine learning, along with their related technological cousins, chatbots and AI, have raised fears among many people that they will one day lose their jobs. In theory, automation and artificial intelligence could liberate people from dangerous and boring tasks so that they can take on more stimulating tasks, make businesses more productive and raise workers' wages. It is true that automation, robotics, and other cutting-edge solutions can prevail without human intervention, but the implementation of these technologies will divert, not replace, human jobs.

Technology has been used in the past to give employees time to transition to new roles. Those who lose their jobs can retrain, claim redundancy or unemployment benefits, or find work in another sector.

Jobs that involve creative problem-solving and creativity - musicians, artists, writers, marketers, inventors - will not easily be replaced by artificial intelligence. Many of these jobs require building trust and interpersonal relationships so that people can relax and be open to what they are doing.

AI provides HR departments the ability to improve the experience of applicant and employee by automating repetitive and low-value tasks, freeing up time to focus on the strategic and creative work that the HR team needs and wants to do. Many professionals turn to artificial intelligence to help them think about problems before making decisions.

Instead of monitoring each step of the new employee onboarding process, these tasks can be automated, allowing teams to dedicate more time to more important tasks like mentoring and feedback.

AI is already being used to automate many HR processes, and it looks like automation will pay off in the long run. From planning meetings to coaching employees today, AI technology streamlines common business processes and eliminates the risk of human error. With this in mind, we should consider seven ways in which AI can improve the efficiency of HR, and one reason why it will not replace humans.

Most experts say that robotic process automation (RPA) will increase efficiency by negating the need for manual processes and data entry. Nearly 60% say RPA will improve the customer experience, and 72% expect humanoid robots to be in use by 2037.

I have not changed my belief that the next wave of innovation will help us maintain our own relevance and add value in the foreseeable robotised economy by harnessing AI's ability to increase our contributions, maximise our potential, and put us on the right track. In this age, human-assisted AI, equipped with judgment and empathy skills and human capital optimization, can measure our learning curve and readiness to enable a continuous symbiosis between individual self-realization and structural changes in industries that are accompanied by emerging needs and skills. The future is murky and it will take effort and evangelization but human resources will play a key role in companies of all kinds, because technology helps teach people how to work with automation and helps us make good use of human-machine cooperation.

While there is a question of whether or not we will be replaced by AI, we can be sure that there will be a time when AI systems will not reach the technical maturity to take over humanity. Today, the complete automation of various tasks is only possible in the human imagination. Before we can answer the question of whether humans can replace AI systems, we need to understand the fundamental differences between the human psyche and artificial intelligence systems.

## Can Artificial Intelligence Augment Human Capital?

Artificial intelligence used to be thought to be the product of science fiction, but most experts now understand that the adoption of smart technologies is transforming the workplace. The use of artificial intelligence in all professions and industries, as well as in human resources, is no exception. A recent survey conducted by Oracle Future of the Workplace revealed that human resources experts believe that AI offers an opportunity to learn new skills, gain leisure time and enable them to expand their current roles to be more strategic for their organizations.

According to Deloitte's Global Human Capital Trends Report 2017, based on a survey of more than 10,000 human resources and business leaders in 140 countries, artificial intelligence (AI) systems, robotics, and cognitive tools are becoming increasingly complex, and jobs are being reinvented to create many of the so-called expanded workforce. In response, organizations are rethinking how they design jobs, organize work, and plan for future growth. According to a study published in the International Research Journal of Engineering and Technology (PDF), integrating artificial intelligence into the human resources (HR) will improve companies by analyzing, predicting, diagnosing and helping HR teams make better decisions.

41% of the companies surveyed said they made significant progress in introducing cognitive and artificial intelligence to their workforce and 34% of respondents are in the midst of pilot projects based on a survey of more than 10,000 human resources and business leaders in 140 countries. Only 17% of global leaders report that they are willing to manage a workforce in which humans, robots, and artificial intelligence work side by side - the lowest attendance trend in the report's five years.

As the economy and data change, companies need to create value to be competitive, and experts predict that by 2030, large-scale artificial intelligence (AI) deployment could contribute to the global economy up to $15.7 trillion. Leaders who want to integrate AI in their organisations need to manage expectations when adopting AI, invest in team building, refine processes and improve their own leadership skills. As AI changes the way businesses work, many believe that work will also change the way organizations begin to replace human employees with intelligent machines.

As machines automate certain routine tasks, the report adds, organizations need to rethink how they work to keep up. While automation will replace human labor, it will also create new jobs and transform current functions.

Because of its original roots and potential confusion with AGI, AGI is reserved for machines that demonstrate the aforementioned human abilities: judgment, common sense, innate creativity, learning, and empathy. In short, the all-powerful full automation of complex workflows requires machines to do most of these things. The prediction is that machine learning of the first order and automation skills for the human cycle will take advantage of machines' unique ability to process vast data sets to expand human capabilities, but the final performance of these systems will depend on humans bringing complementary skills to train and design them.

Ethical use of artificial intelligence represents a new set of functionalities for companies, but the use of artificial intelligence also raises ethical questions about how AI systems should be strengthened for better or worse as they learn. AI understanding will enable machines to interpret, process and learn from external data, based on ideas from human thought processes that can be replicated and mechanized. This is problematic, because the machine learning algorithms that underlie many advanced AI tools are only as intelligent as the data on which they are trained.

AI (Artificial Intelligence) is an area of computer science that allows machines to think like humans. The aim of this area is to focus on machine intelligence in order to solve cognitive problems related to human intelligence. This translates into machine learning algorithms that mimic the cognitive functions of humans and learn to predict what humans would do in the following situation and perform the next appropriate task at the next relevant time.

Artificial intelligence is a constellation of many different technologies that work together to enable machines to sense, understand, act and learn from human intelligence. As a result, artificial intelligence can perform a variety of human reasoning tasks, including learning, problem solving, reasoning, processing and language.

Super teams promise to enable organizations to reinvent themselves, create new values and meanings and give workers the potential to reinvent their careers in ways that contribute to improving their value to the organization and their own employability. In a discussion that culminated in Jobs and Superjobs last year, we examined the rise of superjobs that combine technical and soft skills in integrated roles, combine parts of different traditional jobs and harness the productivity that comes from working with intelligent machines, data and algorithms.

For organizations that see AI (AI) and automation tools as a cost-saving tool, combining AI initiatives with their efforts to build more effective teams is the first step in enabling people and machines to work together in new and more productive ways. There are many certification courses that focus on specific HR topics, and acquiring an advanced degree such as a

Master of Science in Human Resource Management offers students a more holistic approach to understanding the connection between an organization and its employees.

As Barbara Cosgrove, vice president and chief privacy officer at Workday, in a post dedicated to the ethical use of new machine learning technologies, explained ML should not crowd out human decision makers. ML applications that make predictions can be combined with human judgment to make better decisions.

According to research conducted by The Workday, the advent of machine learning and other data-driven technologies present both opportunities and huge challenges for companies to get the skills they will need tomorrow.

# What Will the Future of Human Capital Look Like?

To answer this question, Deloitte published an influential report assessing how companies are responding to the enormous challenges of the technological revolution. According to the report, 88% of the respondents (10,000 entrepreneurs and personnel managers from 140 countries) rated the building of the organisations of the future as the most important. Faced with these changing priorities, companies are changing their way of working and the actual organisation of the company.

New technologies present new challenges for employees and personnel managers. Knowledge and human capital are the foundation of the economy, and the acquisition of talent is crucial for companies. Embedded in the great technological revolution, companies are looking for skilled workers to specialise in emerging sectors of the economy.

The future of human capital management is likely to reflect a growing emphasis on technology and analytics in this area. Human Resources departments need to provide workers with more information and services around the clock in order to save time to focus on employee strategy and career paths. The future of human resources will also include the use of data for strategic decisions, especially when it comes to personnel planning.

Analytics software is designed to collect, process and analyze data on all moving parts of the HR Tech stack. You can use HR analytics software to identify meaningful trends, such as employee training that affects your bottom line, higher-than-usual turnover or candidate quality that leads to future excellence.

This enables a shift from managing talent to building analytical capacities that mine data to recruit, develop, and retain the best people. HR is now a strategic partner for companies when it comes to ensuring that the right talent is available to achieve key corporate objectives. Business partners who can articulate personnel needs to management should consider HR as their internal service provider to ensure a high return on human capital investment.

The transition to a focus of competence requires innovative sources to meet specific work activities and needs, for example as roles change in the gig economy and automation, companies need traditionally equivalent full-time positions previously filled by temporary workers and contractors. When companies manage their workforce, they need to develop better structures to train young talent and select people to advance.

Future trends need careful management of the human capital so that workers feel valued and rewarded while maintaining balance in their lives.

With limited top talent, managers must understand their employees' desire for a balanced life.

For HR managers this means that the future of the work will be to develop a stronger focus on a holistic view of employee well-being that encompasses employees' "emotional, mental and spiritual health as well as their physical health. This will pave the way for new HR roles that focus on well-being as a business strategy to increase employee retention, not just office perks.

For example, the role of wellness director provides strategic wellness management and designs services and practices to promote the emotional, physical, mental and spiritual health of employees. We see companies hiring for this role more often than one would expect more than a decade ago, because we believe that the future of work is also a future of workers' well-being. Work-from-Home moderators ensure that the organization's processes, policies and technologies are optimal for workers remotely.

Human resources experts need to consider how the continued integration of remote work will affect human resources practice. Rochester says, for example, that human resources workers must ensure that distant workers are on time and enforce timekeeping against violations. Organisations with full or partial remote staff must be creative when it comes to employing remote staff and maintaining their corporate culture.

Human resources professionals need to know how to contribute to the vision, mission and financial success of the company to ensure that they are not taken seriously by staff. With a broader range of employee experience, job applications, onboarding checks, benefits, and paid time off available to accommodate digital and customer experiences, younger workers will prefer human resources responsibility to manage these efforts.

Human resources managers should focus on human capital management, training, understanding statistics and job analyses, and outsourcing other aspects of their work to other experts. Contractors and record companies will take on tasks that have previously been done by human resources.

In order to understand how companies are successful, it is not enough to speak the language of human resources. Human resources professionals need to know how to contribute to the company's vision, mission, and financial success, but they cannot take over the C-Suite. On a practical level, they are not able to effectively plan personnel, attract, hire and train the right talent, say experts.

As the Sustainalytics blog notes, it will help overcome the uncertainty of the present and future by getting companies to look beyond their employees and address the challenges and opportunities inherent in the current crisis. The investor community should be aware of the associated risks affecting its portfolios and businesses and the leading role it will play in challenging a company to update its human resources management practices and plans to reap the benefits.

Human capital remains one of the most significant costs of business, often between 50% and 70% of a company's operating budget, taking into account salaries, benefits and other investments in employees and is linked to productivity, innovation and business success. In his letter to CEOs in 2019, Bill Gates emphasized the importance of human capital management and engagement as a priority, sending a strong signal to the business case for caring about the people that make up an organization.

The future of human capital management is likely to reflect a growing focus on technology and analytics in the field, said Jonathan Kestenbaum, director of the New York City-based Talent Tech Lab, a talent-gathering software company. In recent years, there has been rapid technological change and the emergence of new, disruptive business models at an unprecedented pace.

HR departments need to provide workers with more information and services around the clock, and to focus their free time on employee strategy and career paths. It is the technology that will help staff adapt to a changing workforce that is used to going out to appointments and grocery stores.

From now on, human capital won't just be human capital, but augmented, improved, and quantified human capital to be managed at every single level.

www.ingramcontent.com/pod-product-compliance
Lightning Source LLC
La Vergne TN
LVHW010545160826
845677LV00013B/2999

*9798482780282*